# THE PRESENTATION SKILLS WORKSHOP

# THE PRESENTATION SKILLS WORKSHOP

## Helping People Create and Deliver Great Presentations

Sherron Bienvenu, PhD



AMACOM
American Management Association
New York • Atlanta • Boston • Chicago • Kansas City • San Francisco • Washington, D.C.
Brussels • Mexico City • Tokyo • Toronto

Special discounts on bulk quantities of AMACOM books are available to corporations, professional associations, and other organizations. For details, contact Special Sales Department, AMACOM, a division of American Management Association, 1601 Broadway, New York, NY 10019.
Tel.: 212-903-8316 Fax: 212-903-8083
Web site: www.amanet.org



**Library of Congress Cataloging-in-Publication Data**

Bienvenu, Sherron.
The presentation skills workshop : helping people create and deliver great presentations / Sherron Bienvenu.
p. cm.—(The trainer's workshop series)
Includes index.
ISBN 0-8144-0518-5
1. Business presentations. 2. Oral communication. 3. Visual communication. I. Title: Helping people create and deliver great presentations. II. Title. III. Series.

HF5718.22.B54 1999
658.4'5—dc21

99-048052



Printing number

10 9 8 7 6 5 4

# TABLE OF CONTENTS

## PART FOUR: STRATEGIC PRESENTATIONS WORKSHOP HANDOUT PACKAGE 153



## PART FIVE: COMPLETE SET OF TRANSPARENCY MASTERS FOR STRATEGIC PRESENTATIONS COURSE 187

# ACKNOWLEDGMENTS

I developed the material in this book over a twenty-year period, practicing and refining it while working with thousands of people who were preparing and delivering thousands of presentations. Each of these people influenced what you read here. I appreciate their trust in me and their enthusiasm for my process of building presentation skills. This book would not have been possible without the collective experiences of all those clients. I hope they learned as much as I did.

In addition, I would like to thank:

My colleagues at Emory University, Deborah Valentine and Dr. Molly Epstein, for their professional and personal support

My professional associates in The Association of Business Communication and the Management Communication Association for their contributions to the impressive body of knowledge on communication

Michael Hales, who created the original opportunity that led to the contract for this book

AMACOM Books, for recognizing the importance of communication skills training

My editor, Jacqueline Flynn, who read every word of this manuscript, modeling the careful consideration for audience analysis and detail that this book teaches

The reviewers, Maurice E. White, Marcia B. Riley, and Judith Covington, for their insightful comments

My first speech teacher at Centenary College, Ruth Alexander, who taught me about the power of speech

My mentor and friend, Dr. Paul R. Timm, whose encouragement and editorial suggestions on this project were invaluable

My father, Grandison Kemp Bienvenu, who died on April 8, 1999, as I was writing this manuscript but who would have read every word, and my mother, Mackie Turner Bienvenu, who will read every word with her magnifying glass

My daughter, Hillary Reine Tolle, who is my greatest inspiration because she is proud that I am her mother. I have to live up to that.

# INTRODUCTION

Two years into my college teaching career, the governing board of that college decided to consolidate the fine arts departments of its three main campuses. Since I had been teaching theatre and directing drama productions for one campus, all indications were that I was about to be out of a job.

Before making its final decision, the board held a public meeting and allowed individuals to speak for or against its proposal. I took advantage of this opportunity and presented an impassioned plea to leave the fine arts departments near the communities they served. But it was not to be. The vote to consolidate passed.

At the end of the meeting, the president of the college came up to me and said, "Young woman, do you teach public speaking for me?" "No, sir," I replied, "I teach theatre." And he said, "Well, now you teach speech."

So there I was. I had a job, but I wasn't sure how to do it. I had degrees in theatre and broadcasting but not in speech. Most of my work experience was in radio; I had only been teaching for two years. I had just delivered a persuasive speech, but I was just acting on my instincts. And, more importantly, I had no clue how to teach others how to do so. I didn't know where to start.

That was twenty years ago. This book is a result of twenty years of research and application, education and practice, successes and mistakes. I have made the journey to success in the corporate training arena the hard way: by wading through and experimenting with way too much textbook information written by self-proclaimed experts, many of whom had never taught adults in the corporate environment. With this book, I'll save you that trouble.

## WHAT ATTRACTED YOU TO THIS BOOK?

If *The Presentation Skills Workshop* grabbed your attention, you are probably a skills trainer or coach looking for tools to make your people more effective. No doubt you have developed skills and earned credibility as a presenter and trainer. But you may not have the entire skill set or a well-organized package of materials that will translate into success for your trainees.

This book can be a perfect complement to the skills you already have. With it, you can prepare a dynamic and powerful presentation skills course. *The Presentation Skills Workshop* is your complete guide to success.

## WHAT MAKES *THE PRESENTATION SKILLS WORKSHOP* UNIQUE?

*The Presentation Skills Workshop* is a practical guide that gives you all the tools you'll need without forcing you to wade through a mountain of verbiage. The book is designed to be a manual and a guide—not a typical textbook.

The process you will learn works. I can say that with complete confidence, because I have tested and proven it with thousands of trainees from a wide range of organizations. Here are some reasons why this approach is unique:

- The process is designed around and consistently follows an easy-to-remember model.
- The guidelines that apply the model are specific and simple to use.
- The discussion material includes enough theory to support your own personal experience and enhance your credibility, but it avoids academic rhetoric.
- The coaching instructions are easy to personalize for maximum impact on all trainees of any experience level.
- The real-world examples support your own professional experiences as you facilitate the course.
- The worksheets and visual aids are ready to photocopy, thus saving you from reinventing the wheel.
- The program is turn-key yet remains flexible enough for easy adaptation to your training situation.
- The book is packed with stories of real training successes and failures and stuff only learned by doing this a zillion times.
- The style is personal; it is written trainer-to-trainer by someone who has been there, done that.

In short, *The Presentation Skills Workshop* is not the biggest, longest, heaviest book containing everything there is to know about presentation skills training. It is simply all you really want and need to know.

## THE QUICK TOUR

Part One shows you how to prepare to teach the course. It introduces the foundation model that is used throughout the entire process.

- Chapter One presents the Strategic Communication Model. You will teach the course by applying this model. This chapter sets the stage for everything else that follows.
- Chapter Two covers the logistics of course design, including class size, time requirements, and what you can expect to accomplish.

- Chapter Three gets you ready to walk into your training room and launch a dynamic session. It includes checklists and handouts of your slides and worksheets.

Part Two walks you through teaching the course, step by step.

- Chapter Four covers those first critical minutes when you have your only chance to make that first impression.
- Chapters Five, Six, and Seven apply the communication model to the preparation of a speech: doing the "homework" to analyze the situation and audience, selecting and organizing content material, and then creating dynamic visual aids.
- Chapter Eight details speech delivery, including verbal and nonverbal skills, tips for overcoming anxiety, rehearsal techniques, and Q&A pointers.
- Chapter Nine describes giving, soliciting, receiving, and evaluating feedback for continued growth and success.
- Chapter Ten revisits the model looking at male-female communication differences. This can give you an additional edge in managing gender tendencies that may affect both your expectations and evaluations.

Part Three is your follow-up for the course.

- Chapter Eleven includes a sample course feedback form and shows how to interpret your findings to management.

Part Four is the Strategic Communication Course handout packet, complete with ready-to-copy pages and optional examples.

Part Five contains a set of ready-to-copy transparency masters to accompany your lectures and class discussions.

The Appendices provide support material.

- Appendix A is a succinct, generic version of the Strategic Communication Model.
- Appendix B is an application of the model—a detailed procedure for selling your course.

## SO WHAT MAKES A PRESENTER "GREAT"?

A great presenter has two unique qualities: appropriate skills and personal confidence. The confidence derives from selecting excellent information and being comfortable with one's communication skills.

The trainer's challenge is to determine exactly which skills will give speakers the confidence they need. The trainer's confidence comes from the knowllge that the training materials were designed by an experienced, successful, ofessional trainer and that they do indeed work.

Based on my experiences, I wrote this book as if I were talking to you (and metimes as if I were talking to your class). I know your questions and conerns because I've heard just about every one imaginable. I learned most of hat I share the hard way—from the real-world workplace. With this book, I ow you how to master the skills that will make you a better speaker and ainer. The result: You will boost your organization's success and your own by aining great presenters.

# PART ONE

# PREPARING THE STRATEGIC PRESENTATIONS COURSE

# Practicing What You Teach: The Strategic Communication Model

What do you remember about speech classes in school or presentation training at work? Perhaps you were taught rules for preparing speeches that varied with situations, organizational models that changed with the different goals of each speech, and platform skills that were uncomfortable and unnatural. Like most people, you found yourself confronted with too many things to remember, so you picked what worked for you and stuck with it.

Now you will be the one to teach presentation skills. How can you manage complexity in ways people can remember? Where do you start?

Basic rules of training apply. If you are already a trainer, you know part of what to do. If your background is in English or if you are a writer, you know how to teach organizational skills and the effective use of language. If you are trained in speech or theatre, you know how to focus on the audience, demonstrate physical and vocal control, and teach verbal and nonverbal performance. If you have a corporate track record, you can share your business experience and understanding of the nuances of the workplace. You can teach the importance of reflecting corporate culture, and you can model appropriate business platform skills and visual aids.

You probably have an impressive stack of puzzle pieces, but you need a picture to help you put them all together. That picture emerges and powerful training occurs when you apply the Strategic Communication Model.

## THE STRATEGIC COMMUNICATION MODEL

Before getting into the specifics of teaching a presentation skills course, let's look at the Strategic Communication Model. This model is an efficient and thorough five-step, strategic process for professional, managerial, and corporate communication. It forms a foundation for everything that follows in this book. Understanding this model will make you more credible and more persuasive when you present, write, interview, or interact in teams and groups—and especially when you train other presenters. The model reminds you to:

1. **Learn everything you can about the environment** including the current situation, your target audiences, and your objectives with each of those audiences.
2. **Consider your options.** Who should send the message, how should the message be sent, and when should the message be sent?
3. Use that knowledge to **select and organize specific information** to meet your objectives with your audiences.
4. **Deliver your message** with a confident, personal style.
5. **Evaluate feedback** for continued growth and success.

Exhibit 1.1 is a detailed outline of the Strategic Communication Model. Throughout the book, we'll come back to the model with lecture materials that follow the model and cover explanations and examples that apply to the preparation and presentation of your class. (In addition, if you want a complete explanation of the model or would like to hand it out to your class, please see Appendix A: The Strategic Communication Model.)

## EXHIBIT 1.1

## THE STRATEGIC COMMUNICATION MODEL

I. Analyze the Environment
  A. Define the situation
    1. Limit the problem
    2. Assess the external climate
    3. Evaluate the corporate culture
  B. Define your audience
    1. Identify all potential audiences
      a. Primary (actual)
      b. Hidden (indirect but powerful)
      c. Decision maker
        1. Most important
        2. May rely on second-hand information
    2. Learn about each audience
      a. Professional and personal facts
      b. Attitudes about you, your topic, and being there
      c. Their wants over your needs
      d. Consistent concerns
  C. Define your objectives
    1. Overall goal from the mission statement
    2. Specific purpose of the communication
      a. Your needs
      b. Analysis of target audience
    3. Your hidden agenda

II. Consider Your Options
  A. Media options: How should the message be sent?
  B. Source options: Who should deliver the message?
  C. Timing options: When should the message arrive?

III. Select and Organize Information
  A. Review your analysis of the situation, audiences, and objectives
  B. Plan a beginning, a middle, and an end
  C. Focus on specific, personal benefit
  D. Limit your information
  E. Enhance with visual aids, numbers, and examples

IV. Deliver Your Message
  A. Polish your skills
  B. Know your material
  C. Express confidence in your material, your company, and yourself
  D. Be yourself

V. Evaluate Feedback for Continued Success
  A. Give feedback
  B. Solicit feedback
  C. Receive feedback
  D. Evaluate yourself with the Credibility Test
    1. Goodwill: your focus on and concern for your audience
    2. Expertise: your education, knowledge, and experience
    3. Power: your status, prestige, and success
    4. Confidence: how you present yourself and your message

## REMEMBER

The Strategic Communication Model provides a clean, five-step, strategic process for professional, managerial, and corporate communication that will allow you to be more credible and more persuasive when you present, write, interview, or interact in teams and groups. The rest of this book and your entire strategy for training great presenters are based on this model. As a trainer, using the Strategic Communication Model will ensure that you appear focused, organized, consistent, and confident. You will indeed be practicing what you are teaching. Remember:

- Learn everything you can about the environment including the current situation, your target audiences, and your objectives with each of those audiences.
- Consider your options. Who should send the message, how should the message be sent, and when should the message be sent?
- Use that knowledge to select and organize specific information to meet your objectives with your audiences.
- Deliver your message with a confident, personal style.
- Evaluate feedback for continued growth and success.

Your messages will be focused and confident; you will be perceived as credible and therefore persuasive; and you will increase your effectiveness as a communicator and become a great presentation trainer.

# Designing the Logistics of Your Course

One of the most difficult questions a trainer must answer is, Just exactly what will you be able to accomplish with how many people in exactly how much time? Not only must you have an answer, you also must be flexible in response to the needs of your organization. In all likelihood, you will be given more trainees and less time than you would prefer; hence, the need for some logistical guidelines.

## STRUCTURAL ELEMENTS OF A PRESENTATIONS SKILLS COURSE

While you can offer some flexibility, you don't want to diminish the integrity of your course by trying to do too much for too many people in too little time. So before you prepare the content of your course, you need to set your structural parameters by developing a plan of action.

As you calculate, be sure to include the following sections in your presentation training class. Delete the "optional" sections if you are pressed for time. We'll discuss the exact wording in great detail in later chapters.

- **Hold time.** 5 minutes. Wait five minutes to begin, unless you count heads and everyone is seated and ready. Even if they are seated, taking a few minutes to relax and chat among themselves is useful.

- **Logistics announcements.** 5 minutes. Announce break times and bathroom locations. Cover anything that might be unfamiliar to the participants regarding the training facilities. Ask for any questions they may have.
- **Course introduction.** 10–20 minutes. Grab attention, explain basic objectives, and demonstrate specific and personal benefits that participants can expect to gain from the course. Emphasize the "what's-in-it-for-them."
- **Presentation challenge discussion.** 2–7 minutes per person. Depending on how you frame this exercise, participants' answers will take two to five minutes. If you get ahead of yourself and try to respond to each answer, you might use up to six or seven minutes per person. Be careful here and watch your time.
- **Your introduction.** 5–15 minutes. Tell the class why you are qualified to teach this class. The longer your bio and the more stories you tell, the longer this segment will be. Use this opportunity to build your credibility, which is something you will be able to refer back to later in the course.
- **Lecture on the first three steps of the Strategic Communication Model: Preparing Your Presentation.** 30–45 minutes. Again, stories and examples make this longer, but they also make it a richer experience for the participants.
- **Demonstration: video examples.** 15–30 minutes. Optional, but fun and different, especially for an audience that is reticent about participating.
- **Small group exercise.** 30–45 minutes preparation time. 3 minutes per team presentation time. Optional.
- **Individual exercise.** 30–45 minutes preparation time. 3 minutes per person presentation time. Optional.
- **Lecture on Steps Four and Five of the Strategic Communication Model: Delivering Your Presentation.** 30–45 minutes. This part of your presentation includes the fun stuff about platform skills, so it takes longer if you are a "performer" yourself.
- **Exercise: Visual Aid Assessment.** 10–20 minutes. The more examples you use, the longer this will take. Optional.
- **Exercise: The Credibility Test.** 10–20 minutes. Discussion will make this longer. Optional.
- **Individual presentations and evaluations, first round.** Your planning gets tricky at this point. The participants' first speech can be three, four, or five minutes, depending on what kind of presentations they normally give in their work assignments. The more you know about evaluation and the more your participants want to talk, the longer this can be. (See Chapter Nine for more about giving feedback.) As a rule, I assign three-minute presentations to groups of entry-level people and four- or five-minute speeches to executives. Setting up takes a few minutes, and evaluation usually takes approximately three times the length of the speech. Therefore, if you have a class of entry-level employees, allocate at least fifteen minutes for a three-minute speech.

- **First-round wrap-up.** 15–30 minutes. Answer questions, and ask for take-aways. Summarize evaluations, and explain your expectations for the second round of presentations.
- **Individual presentations and evaluations, second round.** These should be a little longer, but you can reduce evaluation time. For lower-level employees, require five-minute speeches, and plan on four per hour. For executives, require seven-minute speeches, and plan on three per hour. This includes setup before each speech and a break after each hour.
- **Final summary.** 15 minutes. At the end of the workshop, participants are likely to feel somewhat drained and are going to be ready to leave. Do a quick round of "what did you learn" and a quick summary of the Strategic Communication Model. Resist the temptation to quit too soon. This kind of wrap-up is very useful to overall comprehension.
- **Course evaluation.** 5 minutes. Ask participants to fill out the form and leave it at the front of the room.

## EXAMPLES OF COURSE DESIGN

It's hard to say which is worse—a class that is too big or one that is too small. I have had some of both, but, surprisingly, the problem with each is basically the same: People won't talk to you if there are too many or too few participants in the room.

My magic numbers are twelve to twenty-four participants in a series of half-day classes with lots of time to divide them into small groups for their actual presentations. For example, in an ideal situation, you would be allocated nine half-day sessions to train twenty-four management-level employees (Exhibit 2.1). But you might be asked to present "refresher" training to twenty-four experienced account executives in a half day (Exhibit 2.2). Of course, this is not a best-case scenario because the participants don't have time to present individually, but it might create follow-up opportunities. We'll also look at a class of twelve entry-level participants in one full day (Exhibit 2.3).

# EXHIBIT 2.1

## NINE HALF-DAY COURSE FOR TWENTY-FOUR ACCOUNT EXECUTIVES OR MANAGEMENT-LEVEL EMPLOYEES

## Nine half days for the trainer

## Three half-day commitments from each participant

**First Half Day** (All 24 participants)

| | |
|---|---|
| 8:30 | Begin (hold for five minutes) |
| 8:35 | Logistics announcements |
| 8:40 | Course introduction |
| 9:00 | Presentation challenge discussion |
| 9:40 | Your introduction |
| 9:45 | Break |
| 10:05 | Lecture on environment, options, organization |
| 10:50 | Video examples |
| 11:10 | Break |
| 11:30 | Lecture on delivery (including visual aids examples) and feedback |
| 12:15 | Summary, four-minute presentation assignment, questions, final take-aways |
| 12:30 | End |

**Second Half Day** (Participants 1–6)

(*Note:* Schedule at least twenty four hours but not more than a week following the first half day. This is a morning example, but of course you can offer an afternoon session. Also, you can easily schedule a morning and afternoon session on the same day.)

| | |
|---|---|
| 8:30 | Begin (hold for five minutes) |
| 8:35 | Announcements about logistics, peer evaluations, video tapes, timing; questions about preparation |
| 8:45 | Speaker #1<br>(Allow twenty minutes per speaker: three minutes to set up, two minutes to explain target audience, four minutes to speak, one minute for Q&A, and ten minutes for evaluation. Then give yourself an extra five minutes of discretionary time for a total of twenty-five minutes per speaker.) |
| 9:10 | Speaker #2 |
| 9:35 | Speaker #3 |
| 10:00 | Break |
| 10:15 | Speaker #4 |

10:40 Speaker #5
11:05 Speaker #6
11:30 First-round wrap-up; assignment for second day
12:00 End

(*Note:* You may choose to replace the one 15-minute break with two longer breaks and run your workshop until 12:30.)

**Third Half Day** (Participants 7–12)

**Fourth Half Day** (Participants 13–18)

**Fifth Half Day** (Participants 19–24)

These sessions replicate the second half day with each six-person group.

**Sixth Half Day** (Participants 1–6)

**Seventh Half Day** (Participants 7–12)

**Eighth Half Day** (Participants 13–18)

**Ninth Half Day** (Participants 19–24)

(*Note:* Schedule these sessions at least two days but no more than a week after the first round of presentations. This is an afternoon example, but you can easily do a morning and an afternoon on the same day.)

1:00 Begin (hold for 5 minutes)
1:05 Announcements about logistics, peer evaluations, video tapes, timing; questions about preparation
1:15 Speaker #1
(Allow twenty minutes per speaker: two minutes to set up, two minutes to explain target audience, six minutes to speak, two minutes for Q & A, and eight minutes for evaluation. Then give yourself an extra five minutes of discretionary time for a total of twenty-five minutes per speaker.)
1:40 Speaker #2
2:05 Speaker #3
2:30 Break
2:45 Speaker #4
3:10 Speaker #5
3:35 Speaker #6
4:00 Course wrap up
4:20 Course evaluation
4:30 End

(*Note:* You may choose to replace the one 15-minute break with two longer breaks and run your workshop until 5:00.)

## EXHIBIT 2.2

### ONE HALF-DAY SEMINAR FOR TWENTY-FOUR EXPERIENCED ACCOUNT EXECUTIVES OR MANAGEMENT-LEVEL EMPLOYEES

| | |
|---|---|
| 8:30 | Begin (hold for 5 minutes) |
| 8:35 | Logistics announcements |
| 8:40 | Course introduction |
| 8:50 | Presentation challenge discussion |
| 9:25 | Your introduction |
| 9:30 | Lecture on environment, options, organization |
| 10:10 | Break |
| 10:30 | Video examples |
| 10:45 | Lecture on delivery (including visual aid examples) and feedback |
| 11:30 | Summary, questions, final take-aways |
| 11:50 | Course evaluation |
| 12:00 | End |

## EXHIBIT 2.3

### ONE FULL-DAY WORKSHOP FOR TWELVE ENTRY-LEVEL EMPLOYEES

| | |
|---|---|
| 8:30 | Begin (hold for five minutes) |
| 8:35 | Logistics announcements |
| 8:40 | Course introduction |
| 8:50 | Presentation challenge discussion |
| 9:10 | Your introduction |
| 9:20 | Lecture on environment, options, organization |
| 10:00 | Self-introduction exercise<br>—forty-five-minute preparation break with refreshments<br>—thirty minutes to present |
| 11:15 | Lecture on delivery (including visual aid examples) and feedback |
| 11:55 | Assignment for three-minute presentations |
| 12:00 | Working lunch |
| 1:00 | Three-minute presentations and evaluations, first six speakers (Allow twelve minutes per speaker: two minutes to set up, one minute to explain target audience, three minutes to speak, one minute for Q&A, and five minutes for evaluation. Then give yourself an extra three minutes of discretionary time, for a total of fifteen minutes per speaker.) |
| 2:30 | Break (and a little flex time, just in case you need it) |
| 3:00 | Second six speakers |
| 4:30 | Summary, questions, final take-aways |
| 4:50 | Course evaluation |
| 5:00 | End |

## MY STORY

One of my goals with this book is to help you avoid wandering into the training quicksand where I have occasionally found myself. This is one of those quicksand stories:

A prestigious educational institution hired me to train a large number of staff employees from a wide range of functional areas. The client assured me that all my participants gave presentations regularly and that they would easily assimilate my material and perform with a high level of proficiency. "And, oh, by the way, we don't have very much money, so could you train forty-eight people in two days?"

I managed to convince them to stretch their commitment to two-and-a-half days. However, since my original proposal had included two presentations by each participant, I organized the five half-day seminar so that all forty-eight people spoke twice, twenty-four at a time in half-day workshops.

Six per hour sounds reasonable, but with late starts, setup, evaluation, questions, breaks, technical difficulties, and a much lower level of proficiency than the client had promised, it was a horrible experience. Everyone felt rushed, and no one was satisfied with the training.

I was disappointed and embarrassed, but I learned a valuable lesson about presentation skills training: When it comes to scheduling individual presentations, schedule at least double the time you really think you need. Participants truly appreciate the individual attention, and their improved presentations will justify your insistence on adequate time allocation. I should have either severely adjusted my program (and the client's expectations) or insisted on half the participants or double the time.

## REMEMBER

Be prepared when someone asks you exactly what you can do with how many people in how much time. Your organization may want to give you more trainees and less time than you know would be effective. Be flexible, but set your structural parameters and be prepared to defend your proposal. Refuse to diminish the integrity of your course by trying to do too much with too many people in too little time. Any short-term gain will be offset by client disappointment and participant frustration. You won't have much fun, either.

# Getting Everything Ready

Congratulations! You've sold your course and agreed with your company about the number of people and the amount of time it will take. Now it's time to assemble your teaching materials and prepare the details.

This is a "make your list and check it twice" chapter. Having the following items well prepared will give you confidence that your program will get off to a smooth start:

- Handouts, including a ready-to-copy participant packet (Part Four)
- Reminder information to participants (see Exhibit 3.1)
- Facilities checklist for your room set-up
- Supplies, materials, and personal details

## STRATEGIC PRESENTATIONS HANDOUT PACKAGE

Your participant handout package should include any or all of the following material. See Part Four for masters for the entire handout package (except for your instructor bio, which you should create yourself).

- Title page—be creative! Part Four includes two generic covers that are ready for you to copy, but I encourage you to create your own cover page for the handout package. Select a design that communicates your distinct personality and style, and include some of your contact information. See Exhibits 3.2 and 3.3 for examples.

- Course description
- Instructor bio to introduce you to the participants. Use my sample bio in Exhibit 3.4 as a model. I created it in sections: academic journals, media coverage, trade publications, consulting and training, and university teaching. Group your accomplishments into appropriate sections. You might have company history, education and additional training, company awards, and training or presentation accomplishments.
- Personal Action Plan sheet on which participants can make notes of information that is particularly relevant to them. Reinforce the instructions about using an idea within twenty-four hours after receiving it.
- Copies of your presentation slides (three to a page with lines for notes)
- Audience Analysis Worksheet. I usually put one worksheet in my handout package and add another one in the back of the binder for easy personal photocopying.
- Outline Worksheet
- Credibility Worksheet
- Presentation Evaluation for trainee peer evaluations. For discussion, just include one evaluation in the handout package. When your class makes presentations, have enough copies for participants to write evaluations on every other speaker.
- Additional readings:
  —Guidelines for Visual Aids
  —Guidelines for Inclusive Language
  —Industry-specific articles. Add these yourself, but remember that you need permission from the publisher to copy articles.

## REMINDER INFORMATION TO PARTICIPANTS

Participants will appreciate it if you send them a reminder memo prior to the workshop. Include plenty of information, even if it may seem unnecessary or obvious to you. Details can be comforting.

Include the following information:

- Date with start and stop time
- Details about the workshop location: a map if it's off-site, parking instructions, recognizable landmarks in the building
- Exactly what they should bring or reassurance that all materials will be provided
- Dress requirements
- Food available

Exhibit 3.1 provides a sample reminder memo.

## EXHIBIT 3.1

## SAMPLE REMINDER MEMO TO PARTICIPANTS

**Memorandum**

To: Selected Participant's Name

From: Sherron Bienvenu, PhD
Communication Solutions

Date: Month xx, xxxx

Re: Reminder: Strategic Presentations Workshop

I am looking forward to meeting all of you on Thursday, Month xx, xxxx, for your Strategic Presentations Workshop. We will start promptly at 8:30 a.m. in Classroom Five, which is located near the center elevator on the second floor of building C. I promise to finish just as promptly at 5:00 p.m.

Your only preparation for the workshop is to start thinking about how you might personally and professionally benefit from a presentation workshop. I'll ask everyone to share communication challenges that relate to presentations, and then I'll address those challenges during the day. Otherwise, all materials will be supplied. Just bring yourself, an open mind, a sense of humor, and an interest in learning!

Dress is business casual, but the room may get cold, so you might want to bring a sweater or jacket.

We'll have coffee, sodas, and bottled water available throughout the day. Fruit and pastry will be served at the morning and afternoon breaks, and the catered lunch will included a choice of turkey, tuna, or vegetarian sandwiches.

If you have any questions, please check with Anne Smart, Training Director, or email me at *drbienvenu@address.com.* See you soon!

Confirm your participant list, and send out your reminder memo. Review the rank and functional areas of participants so that you can check your material for appropriate examples. If possible, casually visit managers and decision makers. Mention that you are about to do this training. Ask for their "ideal outcomes" of your training. Use this information in your class to reinforce needs expressed by participants.

## Checklist: Facilities

Planning a training session is like planning a party: The details can make or break it. Here are some reminders for one to four weeks before your session:

One to four weeks before your session:

- ❑ Confirm your training room location, dates, and times.
- ❑ Visit the room to be certain that it is the right size for your group. Imagine it with tables with ample elbow room, lots of space for you to walk around in, and a table in the back for food and drinks. Make arrangements for the correct number of tables and chairs. Add a couple of chairs just in case interested executives drop in.
- ❑ Order your refreshments. Water, caffeine, and sugar are absolute necessities. I prefer coffee/tea and breakfast pastries in the mornings, sodas and cookies in the afternoon, plus fresh fruit, individual candies, and bottled water all day long. (When I trained at Atlanta Gas Light, the company cafeteria delivered freshly baked cookies every afternoon. We could smell them coming down the hall. It was a wonderful treat.)

## Checklist: Supplies, Materials, and Personal

- ❑ Copy and bind your handouts. Use the best possible layout, paper, copying, and presentation of the handout package to establish your professionalism.
- ❑ Prepare your visual aids. If you are using transparencies, remove them from the paper backing. If they have colored or dark backgrounds, frame them. (Cardboard frames are available at any business supply store.) If you are projecting from a computer, check your slide presentation on the actual computer you will be using because all computers do not read fonts the same way. You don't want to discover after your workshop has started that your computer can't display your slides the way you designed them.
- ❑ Prepare name tents with each participant's name on both sides in large block letters.
- ❑ Decide what to wear. Select a "job interview" outfit. If you need a new suit, buy it in time to have it altered and worn once before the big day to avoid the surprise of a zipper that doesn't stay zipped or a shirt that won't stay tucked. Be sure you are professional looking from head to toe, with a good haircut, manicured nails, nonjangling jewelry, and well-maintained shoes. Your lightest clothing should be worn near your face, which means no white shoes or stockings for women and no bright socks for men. Tie or blouse patterns should not distract. (Your audience should not wonder exactly what that is on your tie.) You should be able to move comfortably in your clothes without having to think about them bunching or pulling, which usually means no double-breasted coats for men and no short skirts for women.

## COUNTING DOWN

Having talked about general preparation, let me get real specific. The last-minute double- or triple-check can mean the difference between a successful launch and a blundering (and embarrassing) start. You will be modeling good communication behaviors before your session even begins. So let's go through two more checklists, even though they may sound redundant.

### ✓ Checklist: The Day Before Your Session

- ❑ Visit your training room and be sure you know how to control the lights and the temperature. Locate the restrooms and phones. Also, review basic emergency procedures: whom to call in a medical emergency, how to get to fire exits, and so on.
- ❑ Double-check the arrangement of the tables and chairs. The participants should be able to see you and your visual aids. Ideally, they should also be able to see each other.
- ❑ Confirm the catering or anything else that is being done for you.
- ❑ Arrange your projector so that you have the largest, most focused picture possible. Your screen should be to the left. (Most cultures read left to right. After your audience members blink or look down, they automatically look up and to the left. Since you are the primary focus of their attention and your visual aids are secondary, you should be to their left.)
- ❑ Check your supplies: handouts, visual aids, flip chart and markers, transparencies and pens (if participants will present on the first day).
- ❑ Review your participant list. Be certain you can pronounce all the names.

### ✓ Checklist: An Hour Before Your Session

- ❑ Double-check everything you did the day before—the room, seating arrangements, equipment, coffee, everything.
- ❑ Pay special attention to the lights. You should be in the most light. Your participants should be able to see to read and write. Try to avoid a distracting glare on your screen.
- ❑ If you are using transparencies with frames, tape a ruler to the top edge of your projector to "bump" the top of your frame against. Your overheads will always be perfectly straight, and you won't have to look back every time you change one. Then mask off any area where light "bleeds" outside your frame. If you are not using frames (your transparencies have a clear background), create a masking tape border on the projector.
- ❑ Lay out your materials in order. Put the supplies you will need later on a side table.

- ❑ Place a handout package, extra paper, and pen at each place. Put name tents by the door to be picked up by the trainees as they enter.
- ❑ Find a place to be alone. Check how you look and talk to yourself in the mirror. Confirm that you are prepared, that you look professional, and that you sound great. Take deep breaths. Stretch. Smile. It's "showtime."

## MY STORY

Working with a U.S. client to prepare for a major presentation to be given in Europe, I worried about everything that could possibly go wrong. I even suggested that his support team transport his visual aids on CD-ROM, on disk, on transparencies, and in hard copy. They laughed at my paranoia, but they humored me.

The competition arrived with one copy of their presentation; their computer crashed; they had to send a follow-up team on an overnight flight to rebuild the presentation at the last minute.

My clients were no longer laughing, but they were smiling very broadly. They were prepared for anything.

## REMEMBER

It's almost impossible to prepare too much. I have never worked in a training room that was perfect; I have always had to move furniture, make last-minute phone calls, or adjust equipment. Usually, I do all of that. My best preparation is to imagine everything that could go wrong and have a contingency plan that would resolve any problem. Check everything, and check it again. Preparation is always a worthwhile investment.

EXHIBIT 3.2

EXAMPLE: OUTSIDE COVER

# Strategic Presentations

or

# (Quick and Dirty) Four-Minute Sound Bite Briefings

Presented to Business Development
Lockheed Martin Aeronautical Systems

Sherron Bienvenu, PhD
*Communication Solutions*

## EXHIBIT 3.3

EXAMPLE: INSIDE COVER

# Strategic Presentations
or
# (Quick and Dirty) Four-Minute Sound Bite Briefings

Presented to
Business Development
Lockheed Martin
Aeronautical Systems

January 1998

Sherron Bienvenu, PhD
*Communication Solutions*
Atlanta, Georgia
770-xxx-xxxx
Sherron_Bienvenu@bus.emory.edu

# EXHIBIT 3.4

## EXAMPLE: INSTRUCTOR BIO

*Facilitator: Use this as a guide to create your own bio. I did this one in sections: academic journals, media coverage, trade publications, consulting and training, and university teaching. Group your accomplishments into appropriate sections as well. You might have company history, education and additional training, company awards, and training or presentation accomplishments.*

**About Your Workshop Leader: Sherron Bienvenu, PhD**

Dr. Sherron Bienvenu specializes in application of theories from management communication and social psychology. Her articles have appeared in *The Bulletin of the Association for Business Communication, The Journal of Business Communication, Management Communication Quarterly, The Atlanta Journal and Constitution,* and others.

Recognized as a communication expert, Dr. Bienvenu is frequently interviewed by media representatives and has appeared on CNN, CNBC, NPR, and CBS, ABC, and NBC-affiliated television and radio networks.

Most recently, Dr. Bienvenu wrote and appeared as on-camera spokesperson in two training videos, "Winning Presentations" and "Winning Credibility," released in early 1998. She also coauthored *CrossTalk: Communicating in a Multicultural Workplace* (Prentice Hall, 1997).

Dr. Bienvenu provides communication counsel for corporations and individuals with expertise ranging from diagnosing organizational communication problems to facilitation of problem-solving and strategic planning. Her corporate clients have included Lockheed Martin Aeronautical Systems, AT&T, Atlanta Gas, MCI, Weeks Corporation, SunTrust Banks, American Cancer Society, Fleet Capital, BellSouth International, Centers for Disease Control, and Vegsauki (Iceland) plus numerous individuals and professional organizations. Her workshops and seminars include a wide range of industries and functional areas: sales, advertising, defense, marketing, healthcare, consulting, broadcasting, real estate, law, education, banking, finance, law enforcement, fundraising, manufacturing, public utilities, and telecommunications.

Dr. Bienvenu began teaching at Goizueta Business School of Emory University in 1982 after a ten-year career in broadcasting and public relations. She manages the school's communication program and teaches professional and corporate communication strategies to BBA, MBA, and Executive Education students. In addition, she teaches Management Communication in the International MBA Program at the Helsinki School of Economics and Business Administration. Her PhD is also from Emory.

# PART TWO

# TEACHING THE STRATEGIC PRESENTATIONS COURSE

# What to Do First (Oh, No! They're Here!)

Just as speakers experience stage fright, every trainer faces some moments of anxiety right before the workshop begins. It's like planning every detail of a huge party and then wondering if anyone will really come. But also like your party, you are prepared, the people you are expecting really are coming, and it's going to be a smashing success.

The phrase, "You only have one chance to make a first impression," not only applies to your first few minutes of class but also gives you a good example for later use in your seminar. The approach for your introduction that I show you in this chapter applies the basic outline and teaches your participants how to introduce effective presentations. Based on your audience analysis and your goals for the workshop, your introduction will:

- Grab their attention
- State your purpose
- Explain your agenda
- Show personal and specific benefit

Let's start with the few minutes before the session begins. You are prepared, and everything is in place—handouts, visual aids, refreshments. Your participants are starting to trickle into the room. Try to greet each individual.

Shake their hands; smile. Since you know who's coming, and you have analyzed your audience, try to welcome them with personalized comments.

If you are experiencing a little stage fright at this point (which, by the way, is perfectly normal), you might be tempted to hide in the hall until all the participants are in the room. Don't! The effort you invest here to establish positive rapport will pay off in countless ways later in the seminar, especially when you ask for participant discussion.

Keep your eye on the clock. While you want to start promptly, plan on five minutes of "hold time." Even if everyone is there, five minutes allows them to relax, chat among themselves, and focus on the class.

When you are ready to begin, stand up straight (good posture conveys confidence) and walk to the spot where you will stand most of the time. This specific movement is a nonverbal signal to your class. Take a deep breath from your diaphragm (yes, you have to breathe) to give your voice resonance. Finally, after all your preparation, it's "showtime."

## GRAB THEIR ATTENTION

When you did your audience analysis of seminar participants, you likely identified several pieces of important information:

- Professional and personal facts
- Attitudes about you, about giving presentations, about presentation training
- Consistent concerns they all share

Among the consistent concerns that come up in almost every seminar are these types of issues that you can address in your opening comments:

- I really don't give "speeches."
- There's too much work going on in my "real job" and not enough time for anything else.
- Training takes too much time while the payback may not be obvious.
- I must be in trouble if they're making me take this class.
- Who are you?

### Lecture: Workshop Introduction and Logistics Announcements

My opening comments for the first half day of the management-level workshop address these predictable concerns and go something like this *(with additional notes for you in italics)*:

**TIME:** 5 minutes

**MATERIALS:** Transparency 1, "Strategic Presentations" (projected on the screen when participants arrive)

Good morning. Welcome to "Strategic Presentations." Thank you for coming today. I expect you have a desk full of work that demands your attention and that you hated to leave. As a result of this workshop, you should be able to accomplish some of that work more effectively and efficiently.

---

*Facilitator: This recognizes a consistent concern about the workshop being a distraction from "real work" and introduces benefits of the workshop.*

---

First things first. This workshop is scheduled to run until 12:30. We'll break at about 9:45 and 11:10, but the coffee is already in the back of the room, and the restrooms are down the hall to the right, in case you need either one before the break.

You each have a packet that includes all the materials you need for the workshop and copies of all the overheads I'll be using. Right now, please turn to the handout: My Personal Plan of Action. Dog-ear it so you can find it easily. As we are working today, when you hear information that is particularly relevant for you, make a note of what you plan to do as a result of this new information. At the end of the day, we'll review your notes. These will be your "take-aways" from the workshop—your personal plan of action for improving your presentation skills.

Before I explain what we're going to do in "Strategic Presentations," here's what we're *not* going to do:

- **I'm not going to bore you with academic b.s. and rhetorical theory.** I reserve the right to throw in a little theory as a foundation for our reasoning, but the focus of this workshop is immediate, practical application for you.
- **I'm not going to give you a bunch of confusing models.** You won't be faced with trying to determine which particular models fit which particular presentation problems.
- **I'm not going to try to change your "presentation personality."** I want you to be yourself and build on your natural abilities. When you stand up to speak, your colleagues will still recognize you.

---

*Facilitator: This acknowledges consistently expressed concerns from participants about unrealistic expectations to make drastic changes in personal presentation styles as a result of presentation training classes.*

---

## Lecture: Workshop Agenda

**TIME:** 5 minutes

**MATERIALS:** Transparency 2, "Strategic Communication Model"

*Facilitator: This material previews exactly what you are going to do and presents an example of the agenda step in the model you are going to teach.*

Here's a preview of today's workshop: For the first few minutes this morning, I'm going to explain some specifics about what you can expect to gain from this course. In doing so, I will address your individual concerns and challenges about preparing and delivering presentations. I'll also tell you a little about myself and why I'm here to facilitate this workshop.

*Facilitator: Display Transparency 2, "Strategic Communication Model."*

*Strategic Communication Model*

- Analyze the environment
- Consider your options: media, source, timing
- Select and organize your information
- Deliver your message
- Evaluate feedback for continued growth

 2

After the first break, we'll talk about the first three steps in the strategic communication model. You'll hear a lot about this fundamental model throughout the seminar; it will provide an excellent guide for all your future presentations. Those first three steps are:

1. Learn everything you can about the environment: the current situation, your target audiences, and your objectives with each of those audiences.
2. Consider your options: Who should send the message, how should the message be sent, and when should the message be sent?
3. Use that knowledge to select and organize specific information to meet your objectives with your audiences.

After the second break, we'll work through the final two steps of the strategic communication model:

4. Deliver your message with a confident, personal style.
5. Evaluate feedback for continued growth and success.

*Facilitator: Turn off the projector.*

Finally, we'll summarize our specific take-aways from today, address any questions, and talk about your individual presentation assignments for the next time we meet.

---

## Exercise: Presentation Challenges

LEARNING OBJECTIVE: To identify the personal and specific benefits that participants hope to achieve in the workshop

TIME: 2–7 minutes per participant

MATERIALS REQUIRED: Flip chart, markers

INSTRUCTIONS TO PARTICIPANTS: Before we go any further, I'd like to hear from you. I'd like you to respond to this question: What do you consider to be your greatest challenge about preparing and delivering presentations? I'd like to start over here and get one challenge from each of you. Then we'll check to see if anyone has any more to add. I think you'll find that other people's stated challenges will remind you of more of your own. You'll also start seeing right away that we all encounter many of the same challenges.

---

*Facilitator: Write the answers on the board or a flip chart so you can refer to them in your lecture on the model. The responses I get usually hit on every piece of the Strategic Communication Model. As you list everyone's challenges, briefly explain how the workshop will help participants handle each problem. Challenges the participants face generally fall into one of three broad categories: content, organization, and presentation skills. The following list includes most of the challenges that participants are likely to mention along with your suggested responses in parentheses.*

---

## Content Challenges

- "I try to cover too much material."
  (**Audience analysis** helps you determine which material is appropriate so you don't waste time on useless information.)
- "I have to present to the assistant first."
  (That situation makes it even more important that your message is focused and clear so that this audience can accurately relay it to the **decision maker.**)
- "I feel like I'm answering the wrong question."
  (We'll talk about a **persuasion continuum** that helps you determine exactly what your audience wants to know and therefore what your **specific purpose** should be.)
- "I make my point too quickly."

(**Support material** enhances a presentation and, of course, allows you to take more time to make your point. Different speakers are comfortable with different types of material, such as stories, quotes, even video clips. We'll help you determine what works for you.)

- "My material is very technical. I think I'm boring my audience."
(This is a universal issue. You have been asked to speak because you know more about the subject than anyone else. Careful **audience analysis,** especially of the audience's level of knowledge about your subject, helps you **select the right information** to keep their interest. We'll also talk about managing multiple levels of knowledge in one audience.)
- "My sense of humor is not always appreciated."
(Use of humor depends on your audience's expectations. Again, **audience analysis** is the key.)
- "I am the youngest member of my group. No one takes me seriously."
(Each person is responsible for establishing the perception of his or her **credibility.** If you are young or female or a minority, it's even more important to include material that builds credibility. I will give you a four-dimension Credibility Test to ensure you are effectively managing the perception of your credibility.)

## Organization Challenges

- "I have trouble getting started."
(If you do your homework first, the decisions about your **opening material** are easier to make, and you will have more confidence when you stand up to speak.)
- "I wish my opening statements were more interesting."
(Audience analysis determines what will **grab your audience's attention.** The Basic Outline Pattern reminds you to include a clear purpose, definite agenda, and specific benefit. Those things make your introduction interesting.)
- "Sometimes I lose my place."
(Of course you do. The audience's brains wander, too. A **great outline and clear visual aids** help all of you stay focused.)
- "I like to write out my speech, but then I read it."
(Notes show your audience that you cared enough to plan ahead, but the notes on your **visual aids** are often enough to keep you on track without additional note cards. We'll talk about the **alternatives to writing everything down.**)
- "If someone interrupts me with a question, first I get defensive, then I lose my train of thought."
(If you establish your preferences for taking **questions** at certain stopping places in your presentation, your audience is likely to abide by your

wishes. If you are still interrupted, a good outline will help you get back on track. We'll also discuss some basic rules for answering questions.)

- "I never feel prepared."
  (**You will feel confident about your preparation if you analyze your audience and situation, determine your goals, and select material based on that information.** We don't feel prepared when we don't spend enough time on the homework.)
- "My visual aids seem old-fashioned."
  (Understanding the **corporate culture** of the receiving department or company will make you more comfortable with the level of technology you choose. I'll also give you some overall **guidelines for visual aids.**)

## Platform Skills Challenges

- "People tell me I talk too fast, but I'm from the North. Everybody talks fast!"
  (You don't have to slow everything down; you'd feel stupid and sound worse. You can, however, **learn to slow down** when you are making a key point.)
- "My knees quiver when I give a presentation."
  (Well, first of all, if your knees are knocking, don't walk out from behind the lectern! Seriously, we'll talk about managing **performance anxiety.** Remember, however, that if you do not feel any anxiety about giving a speech, you have been dead for several days.)
- "I think I sound like a tape recorder."
  (I often ask speakers to talk *with* us, not *at* us. If you don't write it down and read it, and if you speak to us as individuals, you are more likely to **sound like yourself.**)
- "I don't know what to do with my hands."
  (There are lots of options about what you can do with your hands, and only a few things that you can't do. The goal is to be as natural as possible; your **hand gestures** are a nonverbal expression of your personality.)

*Facilitator: You can spend as much time on this as your schedule allows. Go around once, then ask for additional challenges. In this particular workshop, you have twenty-four participants and forty minutes, so you can respond to each comment. Be careful, however, of elaborating too much on each challenge and getting behind schedule so early in the day.*

## Lecture: Workshop Purpose

**TIME:** 5 minutes

**MATERIALS NEEDED:** Course Description in Handout Package

*Facilitator: For a workshop to be successful, your participants should buy in to the stated goals of the workshop. You can accomplish this by explaining the purpose of the workshop in terms of specific and personal benefit to them. For example, talk first about their personal objectives, such as visibility or promotion. Then, connect personal objectives to corporate objectives such as selling more widgets and increasing stockholder wealth, reminding participants that they will also benefit from the success of the company.*

Please look at the handout titled Course Description in your packet. This is my goal. As a result of this workshop, you should expect to develop your abilities in the following ways:

- Identify areas of effectiveness and target areas for growth and development in your oral communication skills.
- Increase your listeners' perceptions of your credibility by understanding target audiences and preparing with a focus on the needs and concerns of each audience.
- Design and implement appropriate and powerful visual aids.
- Improve your speaking confidence through objective evaluation and positive reinforcement.
- Enhance your effectiveness in all career responsibilities through relevant application of communication strategies.
- Realistically assess the impact of your communication efforts on other people.

## ESTABLISH YOUR OWN CREDIBILITY

Finally, as you launch your training session, begin this last piece of your introduction by saying something like: "Before we take a break, I'd like to tell you about my background and why I'm here today. . . ." Refer to your bio in the handout package, but elaborate on the points that your audience would find most interesting.

Remember that the most important element of your own personal and professional communication strategy is your audience's perception of your credibility. If the participants perceive that you are credible—if they believe you, trust you, have confidence in you—you will be an effective trainer.

Credibility contains four dimensions: goodwill, expertise, power, and confidence. You want to be sure that your participants consider you credible on all four dimensions.

1. **Goodwill** is your audience's perception of what you think of them. Audience members need to know that your focus as a trainer will be on them and that you are concerned with their needs. Help them understand that you see them as unique and important to you and your organization. You should have already established the perception of credibility on this dimension from your skillful acknowledgment of their concerns in your earlier remarks.
2. **Expertise** is the audience's perceptions of the facts about you—your education, knowledge, and experience relevant to your topic. You don't want to sound arrogant, but take the opportunity to share the relevant and impressive facts about yourself.

   Make a list of the facts about your education, knowledge, and experience that directly relate to training, presentation skills, and awareness of your participants' organization and industry. Then share that information.
3. **Power** is your audience's perception of what other people think about you. This credibility dimension arises from the audience's perception of your status, prestige, and success. Power can stem from formal position, association with others who have power, the authority you have, and your accomplishments.

   Go back to your bio list and add information about your rank in the company and in professional organizations. Think of stories that illustrate your successes as a trainer or as a speaker. It's your opportunity to mention any recognition that would be meaningful to this specific audience.
4. **Confidence** is the audience's perception of how you present yourself—how sure you are of yourself and of what you are saying and doing.

   Since you achieve the perception of confidence through excellent communication skills, which always include doing your homework and preparing messages based on your audiences' needs and concerns, you should already be doing great on this dimension. Remember the Big Four Rules of Looking Confident:
   - Stand up straight.
   - Look your listeners in the eyes.
   - Be yourself.
   - Smile.

When you finish your self-introduction, announce your break. Be sure to tell participants both the length of the break and the start time.

## MY STORY

The Presentation Challenge Exercise was the result of a particularly disappointing training experience. The training director of the computer technology division of a manufacturing company asked me to present a seminar on managing the media. She gave me a stack of information about the participants and articulated her expectations about the content of the seminar. She also gave me a very tight time slot.

Based on my own audience analysis, I was uncomfortable with the narrowness of the topic, but the client was adamant. Since I had less time than I thought I needed, I just launched into my lecture, using the media as the running example of the participants' target audience.

They looked confused, if not completely baffled. Finally, one participant said, "We don't talk to the press." I suggested that perhaps there would be some opportunities in the near future. "No." They all agreed that they didn't talk to the press.

I complimented them with the possibility of promotion as a result of this training, suggesting that their supervisors surely are confronted with media situations. "No." They didn't agree with that reasoning either.

Any credibility that I may have established was gone. We all suffered through the rest of my presentation. My audience members had decided that there was nothing in it for them.

I will never know why the training director led me into this disaster, but I learned two valuable lessons:

1. If you die in front of a group, you are the only one who looks stupid.
2. Never trust second-hand information.

If I had taken the time to ask the audience about their communication challenges, I could have saved my seminar by addressing the needs of the audience. The opening activities are not just time killers before getting into the real meat of the course. These activities lay the foundation for a successful program. Without a solid foundation, the success of the course is in serious jeopardy.

## REMEMBER

The opening of your workshop is just like the opening of a speech. You have to grab the audience's attention, state your purpose for the workshop, review your agenda, and establish lots of personal benefits from the training. Get people involved from the very start, and they'll reinforce the material you are presenting rather than debate or argue with you.

With a foundation of relevance laid, you are ready to get to the core informational content—the Strategic Communication Model (after the break!).

# First, Do Your Homework

After you have modeled the introduction to a presentation with your introduction to the workshop, you are ready to lecture on the Strategic Communication Model.

The term *lecture,* while correct, sometimes implies one-way communication from speaker to listener only. Don't let this happen. Be careful to maintain a conversation circle with your audience, encouraging comments and questions as you go along.

The following material is my basic lecture, with notes to you in italics. The transparency masters for this portion of your lecture are in Part Five, and the Audience Analysis Worksheet is both at the end of the chapter and in the handout package (Part Four). Use this material as verbatim as you like; the more familiar you become with it, the more you can make it your own.

## Lecture: Preview of the Strategic Communication Model

**TIME:** 2–3 minutes

**MATERIALS:** Transparency 2, "Strategic Communication Model"

Based on the communication challenges you have each shared with the rest of us this morning, it is obvious that you have several things in common:

- **Training.** Each of you has acquired some training in school or at work. You are using what you learned that works for you.
- **Experience.** You wouldn't be where you are professionally if you didn't give presentations on a regular basis. It's simply part of the routine.
- **Success.** You not only give presentations, but you usually give effective presentations. You are usually persuasive, and you usually get what you want from your speech.

Usually. But in today's competitive global environment, "usually" is neither often enough nor good enough. Even the best among us can improve.

*Facilitator: Display Transparency 2, "Strategic Communication Model."*

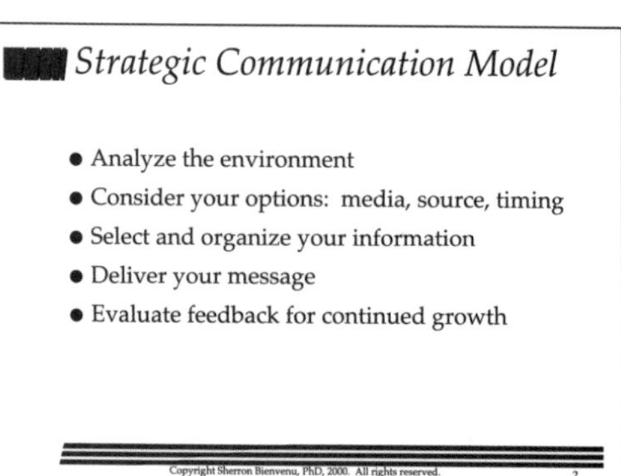


The Strategic Communication Model is a clean, five-step, strategic process for the efficient preparation and delivery of effective presentations. An added bonus for you is that this model also works for all professional, managerial, and corporate communication situations. An understanding of the model will allow you to be more credible and more persuasive when you write, interview, interact in teams and groups, and especially when you present. The model reminds you to:

1. Learn everything you can about the environment including the current situation, your target audiences, and your objectives with each of those audiences.
2. Consider your options. Who should send the message, how should the message be sent, and when should the message be sent?
3. Use that knowledge to select and organize specific information to meet your objectives with your audiences.
4. Deliver your message with a confident, personal style.
5. Evaluate feedback for continued growth and success.

We'll look at these one at a time, beginning with analyzing the environment in which you will deliver your presentation.

## Lecture: Analyze the Environment

**TIME:** 15–20 minutes

**MATERIALS:** Transparency 3, "Analyze the Environment"
Transparency 4, "Define the Situation"
Audience Analysis Worksheet
Transparency 5, "Identify All Potential Audiences"
Transparency 6, "Learn About Each Audience"
Transparency 7, "Define Your Objectives"

*Facilitator: Analyze the Environment is the first step of the model. Take your time with this material, and encourage your participants to avoid any shortcuts in their own analyses. Good decisions about the selection and organization of information depend on this preparation.*

*Facilitator: Display Transparency 3, "Analyze the Environment."*

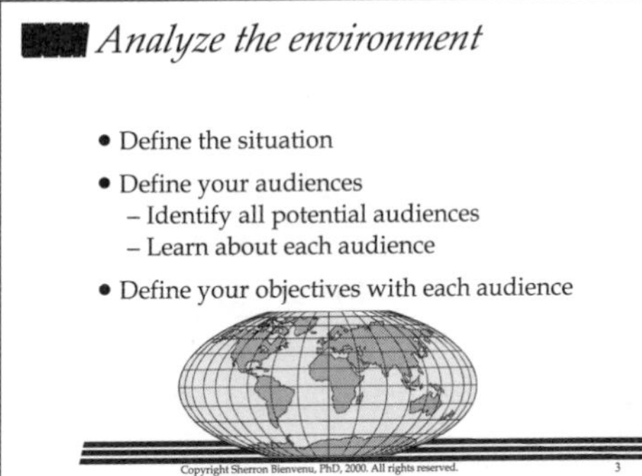


The communication environment includes:

- The existing situation
- Your target audiences
- Your desired objectives with those audiences

Understanding all three of these factors at the beginning of your preparation provides the foundation for the success of your speech. This step is critical for every audience and every situation, such as:

- Persuading clients
- Informing the board of directors
- Motivating subordinates
- Briefing your boss

The communication environment includes situation, audience, and objectives. You must analyze each piece separately, even though the situation, audience, and objectives all function together. For example, the quarterly sales meeting might be the situation that precipitates the preparation of your sales report, and the attendees of that meeting would then comprise your audience. We'll start with the existing situation because the situation often creates the motivation to communicate.

## Define the Situation

*Facilitator: Display Transparency 4, "Define the Situation."*

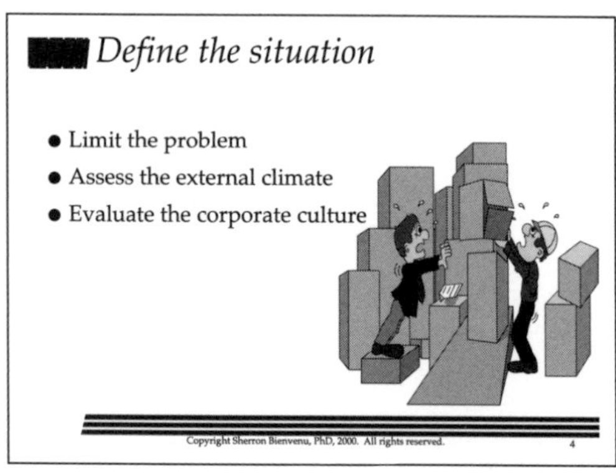


**Limit the problem.** As easy as it may sound, isolating the specific issues that you want to address is often difficult. Focus on the distinct cause for the message you must now prepare. Specify the parameters, and simplify the situation to manageable proportions.

For example, if a labor union in your industry is threatening a strike, you might be inclined to discuss the reasons for the dispute and your opinions about resolution options. A closer examination of the most pressing issue, however, might reveal that you need to address customer service responsiveness in your presentation. The strike threat might be interesting to talk about, but the distinct purpose of your talk must deal with a more focused concern.

**Assess the external climate.** Be aware of what's going on in the specific industry, in related industries, and in the local and global markets that influence the organization and your audiences. Read current industry-related publications; keep clippings. Watch business news. Update your research regularly. Things change fast. Our volatile economies create redesigned industries with evolving cultures.

For example, top human resources consulting firms go beyond standard templates for training companies to manage employee concerns. The best consultants always include both an industry and regional evaluation before they present their recommendations. The baseline processes and procedures might be the same, but the actual implementation varies from, say, a small town manufacturing company in the Southeast to a multinational financial institution.

In addition, many of us are so busy with multiple responsibilities that we either delegate research tasks, over which we might lose quality control, or depend on previously collected information, which might be dated. It's your ultimate responsibility to have information that is current and complete.

**Evaluate the corporate culture.** The culture of an organization derives from the shared attitudes and beliefs that result in shared behaviors. Look at tangible indicators of culture found in any company, including such things as:

- Formal versus informal communication styles
- Professional versus casual dress codes
- Rigid versus flexible work hours

- Flat versus hierarchical structure
- Entrepreneurial, risk-taking versus conservative, "safe" attitudes

Therefore, a communication strategy that would be appropriate in, say, a highly informal, flexible organization might be completely inappropriate in one that is more formal and structured.

*Facilitator: Give an example here that accurately reflects your corporate culture.*

For example, the culture here supports casual, yet technically dynamic presentations. Some of our suppliers are intimidated by too much technical razzle-dazzle, so we should simplify the presentations that we take to their offices. Financial institutions might expect a more formal presentation style; advertising agencies encourage creativity to the point of flamboyance—if the client finds such extremes attractive.

## Define Your Audience

The second part of the Analyze the Environment step includes identifying and learning about the target audiences. Few of us spend enough time on audience analysis, and this step is most likely to contribute details that can make a quality difference in your presentation in a highly competitive marketplace. Often, a speaker's biggest mistake is making generalizations and assumptions about his or her audience. The Strategic Communication Model provides questions to ask about your audiences that will take you beyond generalizing and assuming. We'll use the Audience Analysis Worksheet in your handout packet to answer those important questions.

*Facilitator: Your copy of the Audience Analysis Worksheet is at the end of this chapter. I've also included an example of a completed worksheet. You may choose to use the information on that worksheet as a running example, or you can design an example more relevant to the specific interests of your participants. However, the worksheet is easy to understand, and most people can easily answer the questions about their target audiences without detailed examples.*

Let's take a few minutes to talk through the kind of information you'll need to complete a worksheet on your target audience.

*Facilitator: Display Transparency 5, "Identify all potential audiences."*

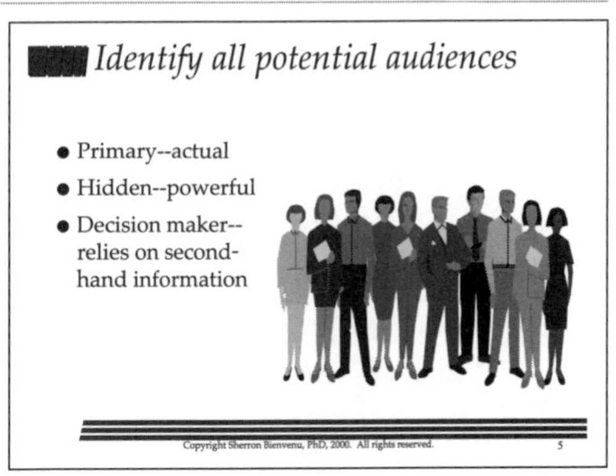

**Identify all potential audiences:** primary, hidden, and decision makers. These audience "memberships" can overlap, and there may be no hidden audience at all, but we need to avoid the risk of neglecting the less obvious ones.

The primary audience is the actual individual(s) to whom you speak. The hidden audience is an indirect receiver of your message. This audience may not be directly connected with the actual communication purpose or process but may have some power over you. The decision maker is your most important audience, even in situations where this audience gets information secondhand from your primary audience.

For example, when clients come to your office for a sales presentation, your primary audience is that group of clients. Your hidden audience might be your manager, who tends to drop in on in-house presentations and who has power over your career progression. Your decision maker may be the executive vice president of the clients' organization who did not attend the presentation but will make a decision based on the reports of the managers who did attend. Therefore, your primary audience must clearly understand your message in order to interpret it later for the absent decision maker.

*Facilitator: Display Transparency 6, "Learn About Each Audience."*

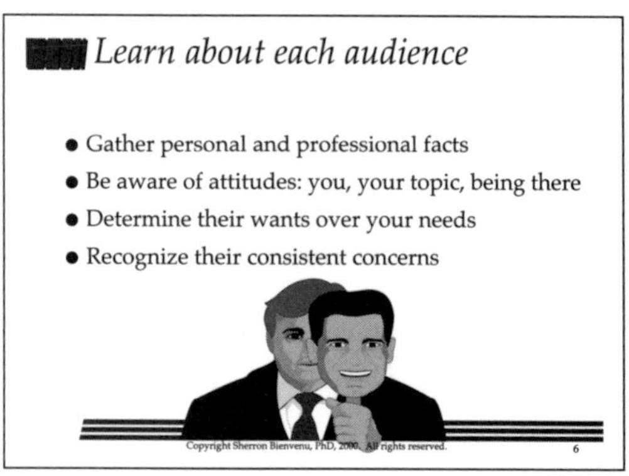


**Learn about each audience.** Focus on facts, attitudes, wants, and concerns.

First, gather both professional and personal facts about audience members such as age, gender, cultural background, education, job responsibilities and status, civic and religious affiliations, and knowledge of your topic. Ask yourself a lot of questions about each listener. Dig for the answers. The longer you have worked with people, the more you should know about them. Review all pertinent information.

For example, be aware that a person's appearance or nonverbal behavior may not tell the whole story. An author once described her acquisition editor as looking and sounding like the stereotypical meek librarian in a 1950s movie. She seemed anything but self-assured and competitive. After negotiating a contract with her, however, the author learned that the editor's hobby was sailboat racing, a difficult, dangerous, and highly competitive sport. The author lamented that she wished she had known all this *before* she negotiated her contract. In this case, a first impression masked a tough, competitive businesswoman.

Second, discover your audience's attitudes about you, your topic, and actually being there as a receiver of your message. Recognition of your audience's attitudes, however, can be humbling. This is the one topic that I'm going to talk about that may not always boost your confidence!

For example, let's say that I'm a presentation skills trainer about to meet the participants in my seminar for the first time, and I'm doing my audience analysis. What are likely to be my audience's attitudes about me? Most of them know nothing about me at all. Hmmm. So what might be their attitude about my topic? Research on fear suggests that many people would rather be thrown into a pit with snakes than give a speech. This could be tough. Finally, what is their attitude about being there for the seminar? They each have a desk full of work, a to-do list a mile long, and the course is required. Ouch.

As disillusioning as it may be, the reality is that many people would rather be somewhere else, with someone else, doing something else than sitting there listening to you give a presentation. Don't try to downplay these facts or hide from the truth. Accept this as good audience data, and face it head-on with excellent preparation.

Third, determine exactly what your audience wants to know. Your job is to give them their "wants" before you ask for your "needs." You must satisfy their information hunger before you ask them to help you convey the important information that will ultimately affect their beliefs or behavior. In fact, one of the biggest communication mistakes is communicating on a "need-to-know" basis. Until you tell people what they *want* to know, they will never hear what you *need* them to know to fulfill the purpose of your message.

For example, the purpose of your presentation may be to explain changes in job responsibilities after a merger. However, employees may not be willing to focus on the details of their job descriptions until you tell them about the security of their jobs or the status of their benefit plans. Satisfy their information needs first.

Fourth, recognize consistent audience concerns. Most people that you interact with regularly express continuing interest in the same issues or themes. Remember to consider that each individual in your target audience might have his or her own consistent concerns.

For example, if you are presenting a budget request to the director of human resources, you are likely to include justifications based on an improved quality of life for employees. However, the same presentation to the chief financial officer might need to be designed around questions about cost. In spite of the importance of quality of life, recognize that the CFO-type audience is really only interested in cost. You are wasting time with issues that your audience considers irrelevant.

## Define Your Objectives

*Facilitator: Display Transparency 7, "Define Your Objectives."*

The third part of the Analyze the Environment step concerns your objectives with each of your audiences. Most messages, no matter how

simple, encompass three objectives: an overall goal, a specific communication purpose, and a hidden agenda.

1. **Overall goal.** The overall goal should be based on the mission statement of the organization or department. For example, the overall goal of an internal presentation about the budget for the next quarter might reflect the company's commitment to increase shareholder wealth. Or your luncheon speech at a civic club might focus on the president's initiative to "give something back" to the community.

2. **Specific purpose.** The specific purpose of the presentation depends on your needs and on your analysis of the target audiences. Pay particular attention to your audience's level of knowledge about your topic. Remember that your primary audience may know a lot about your subject, but your decision maker may need a review of the background information. Ask yourself, as a result of this communication, exactly what do you want to occur? Here's where speakers usually make mistakes: They are not *specific* enough. For example, the specific purpose of the quarterly budget report might be to explicitly explain each department's responsibilities to cut expenditures. The specific purpose of the civic club speech might be to garner support for a plant expansion.

   The process of persuasion can be visualized as a continuum from zero to ten, where zero represents "I know nothing about this," and ten represents "I'm ready to sign on the dotted line!" Business communicators often assume that their audiences know more than they actually do and ask those audiences to move too quickly up the continuum. Work to accurately assess where your audience is, then set a reasonable objective. You can't get from zero to ten in one speech.

   For example, if you determined that you want to hire an additional person in your department, your first objective would be agreement that there is indeed a need. Your next objective might be budget increase or space allocation. Down the line, your objective would be support of a particular candidate. If you started your process by asking for a certain individual, you probably would get nothing at all.

3. **Hidden agenda.** Finally, as you complete your decisions about your objectives with the members of your audience, keep in mind that you have a hidden-agenda, personal goals to which you are aspiring. *Everybody* has them; it is perfectly normal. Each time you present or speak in a meeting, you have an opportunity to work toward your goals. Acknowledge that, and factor it into your planning.

   For example, your hidden agenda could be a promotion to a position with more international responsibility. Include international examples whenever you can. Or maybe you want to be included in more company-wide task forces. Try to select material that illustrates your team skills.

*Facilitator: Use examples that are company-specific, such as selection to cross-functional teams or representing the company at an industry conference.*

## Lecture: Consider Your Options

**TIME:** 5–10 minutes

**MATERIALS:** Transparency 8, "Consider Your Options"

*Facilitator: "Consider Your Options" is the second step of the Strategic Communication Model. Your participants don't really have any options for this class—they must give presentations—but they should understand the pros and cons of all their media choices. In the "real world," delivering information in a presentation instead of a memo or a phone call should be a conscious choice.*

Now that you understand your presentation environment—the situation, your audience, and your objectives—you can explore the how-who-when options available:

- How the message should be sent (media)
- Who should deliver the message (source)
- When the message should arrive (timing)

*Facilitator: Display Transparency 8, "Consider Your Options."*

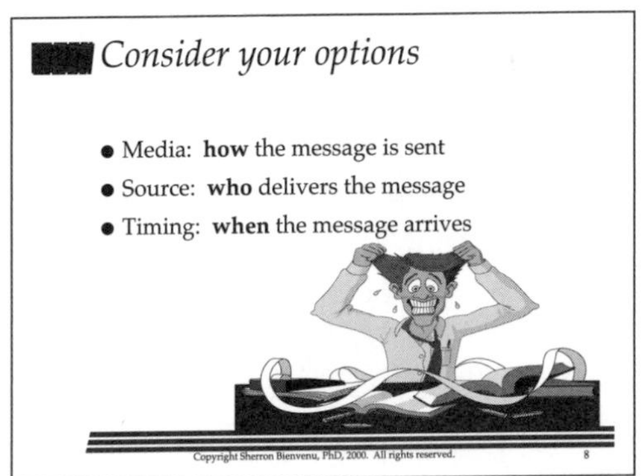


### Media Options: How Should the Message Be Sent?

Obviously, for the purpose of this workshop, you don't have a choice about your medium. You will indeed make a presentation; you cannot fax your notes. However, if you were delivering this information as part of your job, you would want to be certain that it was best suited for a speech rather than for some other medium.

Technology is providing an almost daily increase in media options. In addition to the traditional presentation, letter, memo, interview, meeting, and telephone call, we also have fax, e-mail, teleconferencing, and the ubiquitous "grapevine" from which to choose when deciding how a message should be sent. An effective communicator evaluates the pros and cons of each option in relation to the situation, the audience, and the resulting goals. Some issues to consider when choosing a medium include:

- Personal or confidential content
- Preparation time
- Convenience of the receiver
- Delivery time required
- Consistency of message for multiple receivers
- Necessity of permanent record
- Appropriateness of nonverbal interaction
- Required response time

Unfortunately, we too often make our choices about how the message is to be sent based on our own communication habits—what's most comfortable for us—rather than on the preferences of our target audiences or the parameters established by the situation.

For example, how many of you have a colleague that you avoid calling because that person talks forever, and you can't get off the phone? Most of you. But you may find that individuals who prefer long conversations will not agree to whatever you are proposing any other way. And are there some of you who would rather catch your boss in the hall than write a memo? Of course! But some people are so controlling of their time that if you interrupt them, they are not likely to be agreeable to anything you want. If you write the memos, they will read them on their own schedules, and your request is more likely to get the attention it deserves.

## Source Options: Who Should Deliver the Message?

Again, for this class: No choice. You can't send a proxy speaker!

However, in your everyday work, when selecting the source—the person to deliver your message—the most important criterion is the perceived credibility of that source by your target audience. In other words, whom will your audience perceive as having the most experience, power, and concern for them?

We often make decisions about the source based on our own needs rather than those of the receiver. For example, we naturally take ownership of a project and then want to personally see it through to completion by presenting it to supervisors, clients, and other decision makers. In truth, however, someone else may be more effective in presenting your message.

In addition, if you have multiple audiences, you might appeal to them with multiple speakers, each selected for his or her perceived credibility with the targeted receiver of the presentation. The rules for preparing team presentations are the same as for individual presentations, except that it is even more important to develop succinct internal summaries and clear transitions.

## Timing Options: When Should the Message Arrive?

Again, consider the needs of your audience in conjunction with your own communication goals when deciding when to present the message. We too often communicate at our own convenience, which may not be convenient for our audience. Remember that time itself is interpreted differently in other cultures and that time itself conveys meaning.

For example, simply arriving at this class on time sends a message that you are dependable and enthusiastic. Your willingness to volunteer to deliver your presentation first could be saying that you are brave or that you want to get it over with!

Additional considerations are sequencing and spacing, particularly with multiple audiences receiving different messages. For example, your choices about the people you greet when you arrive and how long you speak to them send messages about your priorities.

Complex messages designed for several different audiences require careful scrutiny. Decide which audience is to receive which message in what order. Also consider how much time to allow between messages. The very process of selecting which audience to tell first communicates a strong message in itself.

For example, if you decide you want to roll out a new product to each of your divisions across the country by personally speaking to each group, you must consider the consequences. Which group do you tell first, and how will the order of your visits be perceived? There is often not a concrete solution to that problem, but at least you can address the negative perceptions.

*Facilitator: Turn projector off.*

## MY STORY

*Facilitator: I suggest that you offer an example about your own experience or perhaps that of a client. The following is one that I often use.*

One of my regular clients—let's call him Bob—called me in to help him structure a presentation that he had been asked to give to the new president of the company, whom we'll call George. I started with my usual audience analysis questions about George's background. Bob knew very little information, but he was adamant about the grapevine's information that George liked a lot of detail. As a result, Bob wanted to load up his presentation with lots of words on lots of slides.

I was not comfortable with this decision and suggested that a bio of the new president must be available on the company website. It was. George was an engineer with an MBA from MIT, which is one of the most quantitative master's programs in the country. As a result of this information, Bob substituted graphs for words and created a presentation that was successful with his new boss.

## Lecture: Summary of "First, Do Your Homework"

**TIME:** 2 minutes

*Facilitator: You are modeling the summary and action steps of the basic outline with this "remember" statement at the end of your lecture. This answers the questions: What do you want them to remember? and What do you what them to do?*

Always do your homework. First, learn everything you can about the environment: the current situation, your target audiences, and your objectives with each of those audiences. Then, consider your options: Who should send the message, how should the message be sent, and when should the message be sent? We'll use that knowledge to select and organize specific information to meet your objectives with your audiences.

*Facilitator: Ask for questions here. The one you are likely to receive is about the time it takes to fill out the Audience Analysis Worksheet. Assure your class that completing the worksheet should take only ten to fifteen minutes the first couple of times they do it. However, many of the questions are things they think about all the time, so the task will get faster as they get used to it. The challenge is in identifying the questions that an individual consistently forgets to ask and then remembering to ask that question about each target audience. Remind them of the author who forgot to assess the personal characteristics of her acquisitions editor.*

WORKSHEET

# AUDIENCE ANALYSIS

Who is my primary audience (actual receiver of my presentation)?

______________________________________________

What do I know about him/her/them personally and professionally (age, gender, education, job responsibility and status, civic and religious affiliation, knowledge of subject, cultural background)?

______________________________________________

______________________________________________

What is his/her/their attitude about me?

______________________________________________

About my subject?

______________________________________________

About being there to listen to my presentation?

______________________________________________

What does my audience *want* to know about my subject?

______________________________________________

What do I *need* my audience to know?

______________________________________________

What is the *consistent concern* that I always hear from my audience?

______________________________________________

What specific information addresses that concern?

______________________________________________

______________________________________________

Who is my hidden audience?

_______________________________________________

What do I know about him/her/them?

_______________________________________________

_______________________________________________

What is the *consistent concern* of my hidden audience?

_______________________________________________

What specific information addresses that concern?

_______________________________________________

_______________________________________________

Who is the decision maker?

_______________________________________________

What do I know about him/her?

_______________________________________________

_______________________________________________

What is the *consistent concern* of the decision maker?

_______________________________________________

What specific information addresses that concern?

_______________________________________________

_______________________________________________

Other observations:

_______________________________________________

_______________________________________________

_______________________________________________

WORKSHEET

# AUDIENCE ANALYSIS EXAMPLE

***(Note and disclaimer: This hypothetical example was based on Internet and newspaper articles and developed as a class exercise.)***

Speaker: BigMag Sales Manager

Who is my primary audience (actual receiver of my presentation)?
*Current BigMag sales team*

What do I know about them personally and professionally (age, gender, education, job responsibility and status, civic and religious affiliation, knowledge of subject, cultural background)?
*Diversity in all areas; limited knowledge of the upcoming joint venture with HugeCorp*

What is their attitude about me?
*Open, because they know I have information that they need*

About my subject?
*Skeptical, because they want to know how the joint venture will affect their jobs*

About being there to listen to my presentation?
*Curious, perhaps anxious, because they have been worried and would like to know what the future holds for them and for the company*

What does my audience *want* to know about my subject?
*What's in this joint venture for them? Will jobs be cut, or will employees get more benefits?*

What do I *need* my audience to know?
*I need the sales force to be informed about the change in corporate strategy and about the additional products they will be selling in the future*

What is the *consistent concern* that I always hear from my audience?

*Will this joint venture threaten job security?*

What specific information addresses that concern?

*Employee jobs will remain secure because:*

- *BigMag will remain an equal partner with HugeCorp (each company will maintain separate operations)*
- *Employees may have to sell additional items, which may mean a larger sales force and more job opportunities*
- *The joint venture will likely increase the company profits, which should result in more income and benefits for employees*

Who is my hidden audience?

*Top management of BigMag*

What do I know about them?

*Management is enthusiastic about the joint venture and believes it to be a profitable investment*

What is the *consistent concern* of my hidden audience?

*Management wants to ensure that the sales team is excited and motivated by the joint venture; they know that sales drive profits*

What specific information addresses that concern?

*By addressing the concerns of the sales team, I can get them excited and motivated*

Who is the decision maker?

*Each person in the room; the BigMag Sales team (see info for primary audience)*

# Get the Words in Order

After taking questions about the "homework" sections of the model, it's time to discuss how to use research to design the presentation. Your participants will be eager to get to this part; your comments about "using this fact or that information when actually selecting material" will have prepared them for what's to come.

The following material, once again, is my basic lecture, with additional notes to you in italics.

---

## Lecture: Selecting and Organizing Information

**TIME:** 3 minutes

**MATERIALS:** Transparency 9, "Select and Organize Information"
Outline Worksheet

Now that you have discovered everything you can learn about your current situation, target audiences, and objectives with those audiences, and you are certain that this particular message should be a presentation delivered by you, it's time to make some decisions about selecting and organizing material.

A common mistake of inexperienced speakers is to start preparing at this point. We are given an assignment to make a presentation, and we immediately start selecting and organizing information. We try to avoid the requisite first two steps in the model (Analyze the Environment and Consider your Options). Since communication is at least 50 percent common sense, you may be able to get by with a lack of analysis once in a while. However, in our current business environment, "getting by" does not provide you with a competitive advantage. And misdirecting information because of weak analysis of the environment and audience can seriously damage a speaker's credibility.

*Facilitator: Display Transparency 9, "Select and Organize Information."*

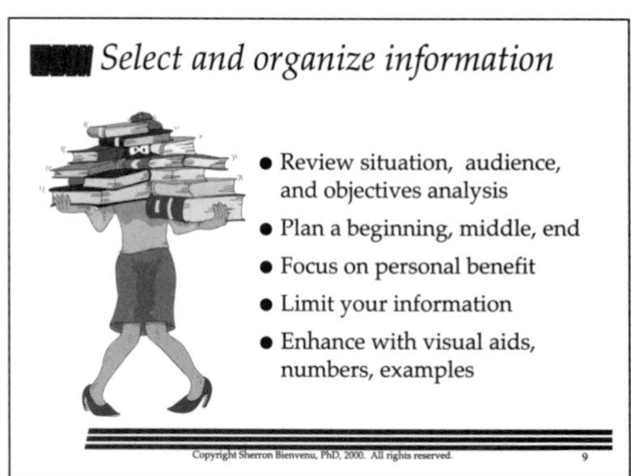


First of all, review your analysis of your situation, your target audiences, and your objectives with those audiences. Have your Audience Analysis Worksheet handy for easy reference. As you plan the beginning, middle, and end of your presentation, focus on material that offers specific, personal benefit to your audience. Excluding irrelevant material that focuses on your own benefit is one of the best ways to limit your main points. Finally, prepare appropriate visual aids, and add illustrations or examples that will appeal to your audience.

Let's look at organization in terms of the three main parts of your presentation:

1. The beginning (Introduction)
2. The middle (Body)
3. The end (Conclusion)

If this sounds like "tell them what you're going to tell them, then tell them, then tell them what you told them," it is. This basic organization plan really works. The purpose is to reinforce, not to be unnecessarily redundant. A consistent, reinforced message ensures that listeners will grasp the purpose of your communication.

Unfortunately, too many speakers choose another option, which is an introduction that consists of "Hello, my name is John, and I'm here to talk about the budget." The body consists of at least ten main points, which no one can remember. And the conclusion is "Are there any questions," followed by "Thank you."

*Facilitator: Choose a different name if there is a John in your group or on the senior executive staff!*

Of course there are no questions because the audience lost track so many times that they wouldn't dare ask a question for fear that the material really had been discussed. Instead, the audience claps wildly, but their gleeful appreciation is because the speech is over!

The Outline Worksheet in your handout packet asks the appropriate questions to guide you through the process of creating the introduction, body, and conclusion of a presentation. You might want to refer to that as we discuss this part of your preparation.

*Facilitator: Your copy of the Outline Worksheet is at the end of this chapter. I've also included an example of a completed worksheet, based on the Audience Analysis Worksheet in Chapter Five. You may choose to use the information on that worksheet as a running example, or you can design an example more relevant to the specific interests of your participants. However, the worksheet is easy to understand, and most people can easily answer the questions without detailed examples.*

## Lecture: The Introduction

**TIME:** 7–10 minutes

**MATERIALS:** Transparency 10, "Basic Outline"

*Facilitator: Display Transparency 10, "Basic Outline."*

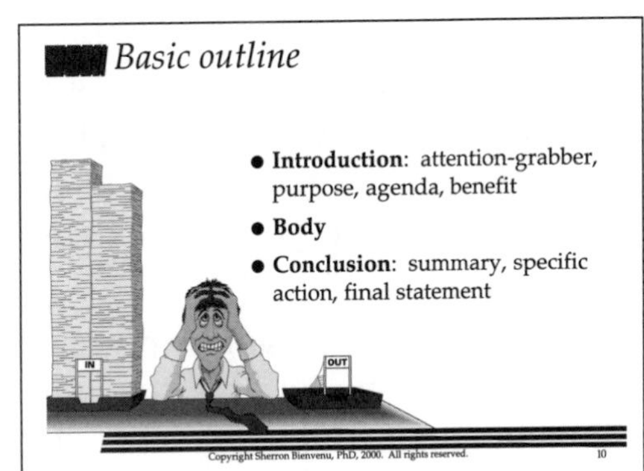


You must accomplish four objectives in your introduction:

1. Grab your audience's attention.
2. State your purpose.
3. Explain your agenda.
4. Establish personal benefit.

With the exception of grabbing attention, these are not steps that must follow a particular order. But you must do all of them. If you are clever and succinct, you can even accomplish several objectives in just one sentence.

## Grab the Audience's Attention

The question you ask yourself is: Based on what I know about my primary audience, what will get their attention? There are lots of ways to grab attention. What grabs your attention? What kinds of things work for you in your own presentations? What have you heard other people do that worked for them?

*Facilitator: As participants make suggestions, respond with the pros and cons associated with that particular attention-grabber. Then add the ones they leave out. Ask participants for examples of each type of attention-grabber.*

- **A joke.** Contrary to popular belief, this is probably not the best choice of attention-grabber. Humor can be very effective, but it is hard to deliver well. A joke can sound contrived or just not be funny. And fairly often, a joke is told at someone's expense, and it will be your luck that the person you are offending is the very person who signs your check. But almost every audience in almost every situation appreciates a witty speaker with a sense of humor. You might tell a humorous story on yourself (this is safer than one that makes fun of someone else), but be wary of too much self-deprecation, which can hurt your credibility.
- **Something startling.** Maybe, if it relates to your speech. A frightening statistic about the percentage of workplace accidents can be very effective to open a speech about the cost of workman's comp. But a loud noise that startles without tying to the topic is not likely to make an effective introduction (unless, of course, your topic is something like noise as a distraction in the office).
- **A great story.** Yes, if you have told the story before and are good at this. Some people are wonderful storytellers. Most people can tell stories, but some have trouble sounding spontaneous. Be careful to keep the story brief. You don't want your introduction to be longer than the body of your speech, and a story can get away from you.
- **A picture or visual aid.** This aid can grab attention if it is clear and easy to see. An object must be big enough to be seen by the entire audience; a picture must require no explanation.
- **A question.** Often the best idea for insecure speakers with limited time. With a question, you can grab attention, state your purpose, and establish personal benefit, all in just a few words such as, "Would you like to double your salary in the next five years?" Be sure you have thoroughly analyzed your audience, however. You wouldn't want to ask a quality-of-life question to the audience who only cares about the bottom line. Often such questions are rhetorical—you don't really expect an answer.

## State Your Purpose

Ask yourself: As a result of this message, what do I want my audience *to do*? Review your audience analysis and your decisions about your objectives for your audience, remembering that you can usually only move your audience up a couple of steps on the persuasive continuum. If your audience knows very little about your proposed project, your goal might be to explain the project and establish the need. If they are aware of the need and how your project will provide a solution, you might ask for budget allocation.

In addition, consider if there are any reasons that you should be *indirect* with the purpose of this message. If so, how should you temper your expressed goals? For example, let's say the purpose of your presentation is to announce the negative impact of the budget cutbacks, such as fewer support personnel, less discretionary funds, etc. You might want to carefully explain the reasons before giving such bad news, so your stated purpose in your introduction would simply be "to explain the budget decisions for next year."

### Explain Your Agenda

Ask yourself: How am I going to accomplish my objectives—that is, what is my *agenda* for delivering the message? The agenda is a roadmap, both for you and your audience. It keeps everyone on track. For example, the agenda statement for your budget presentation might be: "I'm going to discuss the criteria for the budget decisions, the actual decisions, and how those decisions will affect you." Be explicit about your agenda, and the audience will clearly understand where you are going.

### Establish Personal Benefit

Ask yourself: What's in it for them, *specifically* and *personally?* Focus on specific, personal benefit for the individuals receiving the message. Also include benefit to the department or organization, but be careful not to just talk about these organizational benefits. People always want to know about personal relevance.

For example, an audience of employees wants to know how your proposal will make employees' jobs easier or increase their income. You might expect these employees to be interested in profit and shareholder wealth, but in their hearts, they really want to know what's in it for each of them, specifically and personally. So, "If we do this, the company will make more money" is simply not enough to persuade employees to support your proposal.

---

## Lecture: The Body

**TIME:** 7–10 minutes

**MATERIALS:** Transparency 11, "Decision-Making Pattern"
Transparency 12, "Bad News Pattern"
Transparency 13, "STARR Pattern"

There are three basic things to keep in mind when you start to work on the body of your presentation:

1. Select an appropriate organizational pattern.
2. Limit your information.
3. Support your presentation with stories, numbers, and examples.

## Select an Appropriate Organizational Pattern

Based on your analysis of your audience and your decisions about objectives with your audience, choose an organizational plan that best meets your needs. Some material will work in several organizational patterns, so you might want to consider more than one pattern for "fit" before you make your final decision. Here are some options, most of which you will recognize:

- Chronological order for simple, ordered instructions or reports
- Problem (three parts) and solution (one part) for audiences with low knowledge of the issues
- Problem (one part) and solution (three parts) for audiences with high knowledge of the issues
- Current situation and proposed situation for many persuasive presentations
- Inductive (general to specific) or deductive (specific to general) reasoning for explanations
- Pros and cons (or compare and contrast) for simple analyses or evaluations
- Decision-making pattern for complex issues
- Bad-news pattern for information the audience does not want to hear
- STARR (situation, task, action, results, recommendations) pattern for reporting situation, task, action, result, and recommendations

*Facilitator: Four of these patterns usually require more explanation, which you can add as you go through your list or at the end.*

**Problem-solution pattern.** For most persuasive presentations, the problem-solution format works the easiest. If your audience is low on the persuasive continuum—if they have little knowledge about the issue—you will want to spend more time explaining the specifics of the problem. If your audience knows all about the problem, you can spend the majority of your time considering a choice of solutions.

*Facilitator: Display Transparency 11, "Decision-Making Pattern."*

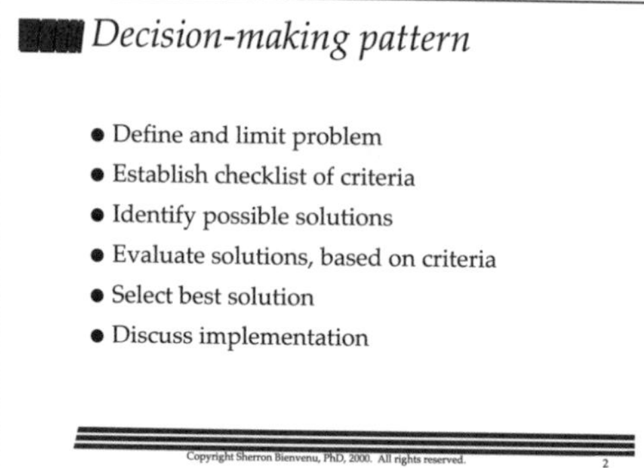


**Decision-making pattern.** This outlining strategy reminds you to explain the criteria you used when determining how to solve your problem. If you establish criteria first, then show how potential solutions measure up against those criteria, your decision develops its own support as you move through your presentation.

*Facilitator: Display Transparency 12, "Bad News Pattern."*

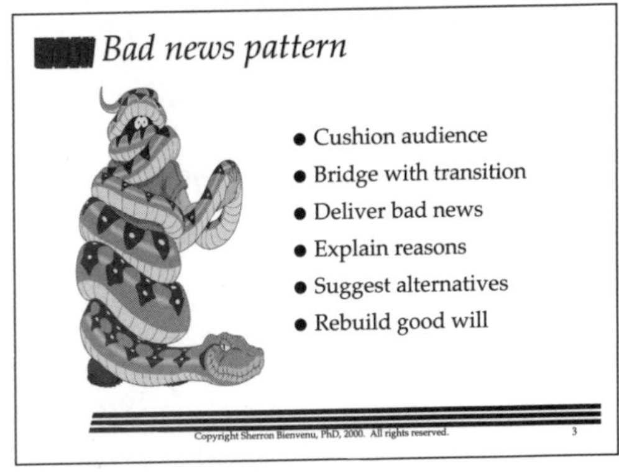


**Bad news pattern.** When giving people information that they would rather not hear, select the bad news pattern. This organizational strategy allows you to buffer the bad news with a neutral or mildly positive statement first. Be careful that the material you choose is appropriate for the message that is coming; you don't want to compliment them on being "perfect" employees and then fire them.

The "deliver bad news" and "explain reasons" steps are interchangeable. Some speakers would rather get the bad news over with and then explain, while others would rather explain first. Whichever way you choose, it is most important that you offer good reasons. "It's company policy" is not enough.

The bad news pattern includes alternatives—specific replacements for whatever it is they want but you cannot give. For example, an important client may have requested that certain products be delivered by specific dates. If you are unable to meet the request, your alternatives might be to deliver a slightly different product on the date requested or to discount the price to offset late delivery. Offering alternatives almost always reduces the sting of bad news.

Complete the bad news pattern by rebuilding goodwill with your audience, thus sandwiching the negative information between positive, audience-focused material.

*Facilitator: Display Transparency 13, "STARR Pattern."*

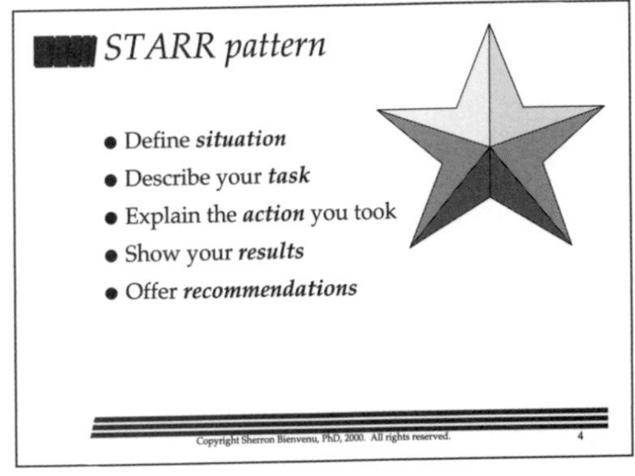


**STARR pattern.** STARR is an acronym for situation, task, action, results, and recommendations. This organizational strategy keeps you from leaving out important information. Some speakers neglect the set-up that an audience needs to know (What is the situation? What was your specific task?). Others forget to tell the audience what they *want* to know (What were the results? What are your recommendations?). An additional benefit of the STARR pattern is that it will work if you only have two minutes in the elevator with your boss, and you want to offer an update on your current project. Memorize the five STARR points and use them for instant organization, especially when someone puts you on the spot for a quick response.

*Facilitator: Turn off projector.*

## Limit Your Information

As you consider material that will develop your arguments, stay focused on your original objective. Restrict your agenda to one specific situation or problem. Avoid wandering off to discuss other items that may be on your personal agenda but are not relevant to your stated purpose.

Cognitive psychologists tell us that people can remember between three and seven items. Busy business people are more likely to remember only three.

If you give your audience too many reasons to buy your product or implement your idea, they may only remember a few of them, which may not be your most persuasive points. Therefore, even if you have a lot of points to cover, group them. For example, a new marketing process may actually comprise eleven or twelve steps, but you can group them into categories such as design steps, packaging steps, and sales steps. In a problem-solution pattern, there might be seven individual problems. Grouping them into personnel problems and logistics problems would make your presentation easier to follow and remember.

## Enhance with Stories, Numbers, and Examples

No matter how brilliantly you speak, your audience will remember your points better when supported with appropriate pictures and stories. This is another place where your audience analysis will really pay off. For example, if you know that your decision maker is an avid baseball fan, you might choose baseball metaphors to illustrate your points ("We'll hit a home run with this product."). Just be careful that you have your metaphors straight, and avoid such blunders as "if the ball's in your court, pick it up and run with it!"

Take your cues from every detail about your audience that is available, being careful not to inject too much of your own personal knowledge, especially if what you do for fun is somewhat different from the norm. For example, a manager whose hobby was ballroom dancing used to say, "In the dance of life, few people are brave enough to tango." Few people got it. Her clever metaphor was wasted.

Even though most people agree that stories and examples are one of the most effective devices in a memorable presentation, they can also be the most difficult for speakers who struggle with spontaneity. However, if you keep your narrative short and focus on benefit for your audience, your story will be a success.

## Lecture: The Conclusion

**TIME:** 3–5 minutes

**MATERIALS:** Transparency 10, "Basic Outline"

*Facilitator: Display Transparency 10, "Basic Outline" again.*

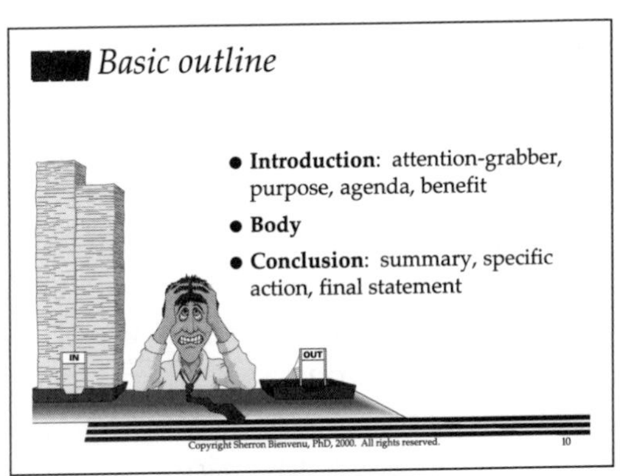


Your conclusion should accomplish the following three things:

1. Summarize your main points.
2. Ask for specific action.
3. Close with a strong final statement.

### Summarize Your Main Points

This is a place in the presentation where speakers who cut corners will jeopardize the effectiveness of all their preceding work. The two most common mistakes are:

1. Listing the main topics instead of summarizing them
2. Summarizing only some of your main points, such as the solution or the recommendations

For example, let's go back to the budget presentation we discussed earlier. If you *listed* the main topics instead of summarized them, you might say, "I've discussed the criteria for the budget decisions, the actual decisions, and how those decisions will affect you." If you summarized only *some* of your main points, you might say, "You should remember that this affects both your support personnel and your discretionary funds." A *complete summary* would cover the essence of all the points: "I'd like you to remember that the budget decisions were based on the rising cost of raw materials and labor in this increasingly competitive market. The bottom line decision is to cut all expenditures by 3 percent. We expect this cut to hit your department the hardest in terms of raises for your support personnel and your discretionary funds." Summarize the most important information from each main point.

### Ask for Specific Action

Exactly what do you want them to do? Tell them. Be specific. Don't ask them to think about some ways to reduce costs. Instead, ask them to prepare a list of ten specific areas or projects where 3 percent could be trimmed. Tell them that you would appreciate receiving that list by a week from Friday. Be very clear.

## Close with a Strong Final Statement

Think carefully about your last words, since they could be what your audience remembers best. Avoid at all costs making these closing statements awkward, inappropriate, or insincere. "Thank you" is not a strong final statement, even though many audiences expect a "thank you" as a signal that you are finished.

"Are there any questions" is not a strong final statement, either. In fact, never wait until the very end to ask for questions. Doing so exposes you to the risk that the last question you take will be the one you are not prepared to answer, and then your last words will be clumsy. Ask for questions before or after your summary so your last words will be a strong, prepared wrap-up.

The best trick for making a final statement memorable is to repeat some element of your attention-grabber—a startling fact, a great story, a dramatic picture. However, since your final statement is your last impression on your audience, consider material that will show the most benefit for them and will have the greatest impact on your objective. For example, if you started your presentation with a negative illustration of the problem you were going to address in your speech, you might close with a similar but positive illustration of your solution.

*Facilitator: Turn off projector.*

## MY STORY

*Facilitator: One way to summarize the use of the outline is to tell a story about how you applied it yourself. If you can adapt a personal situation, by all means use your own story. Otherwise, try the following one.*

Shortly after I started teaching college, I had an opportunity to use the basic outline worksheet for a corporate client who had called in a panic about a speech she was giving for a conference of stock brokers. Based on her success selecting a particular mutual fund, her assigned objective was to entice her peers to sell that fund to their respective clients. She had stacks of material and a fifteen-minute time slot on the program.

I suggested that she put all her material away and get out one piece of paper. She thought I had lost my mind. Her original plan was to write everything down, word for word. Instead, I went through the list of questions on the Audience Analysis Worksheet and the Outline Worksheet in your handout package. She carefully considered her audience and selected material that appealed to the needs of that audience. After the outline was completed, I asked her if she could tell me a story or show me a graph that illustrated each of her main points. Of course she could, and she did without a thought to needing notes. She left my office with her speech outline on one piece of paper.

Three days later, she sent my check and the biggest basket of flowers I had ever seen. The card read, "I was better than I ever thought I could be. I was prepared and confident. I did great. Thank you."

I knew for sure then that using a specific outline really works. It always will.

## Lecture: Summary of "Get the Words in Order"

TIME: 1 minute

Always review your analysis of your audience and your situation.

- In your introduction: Grab your audience's attention, state your purpose, explain your agenda, and establish personal benefit.
- In your body: Select an appropriate organizational pattern, limit your information, and support your points with great stories, numbers, and examples.
- In your conclusion: Summarize the essence of your main points, ask for specific action, and close with a strong final statement.

Do all the steps of organization each time you prepare a talk. They will become more natural—more a part of your presentation style—as you become more and more effective as a speaker.

*Facilitator: Check for questions here. You might have to review the points of the introduction and conclusion or the organizational patterns for the body.*

## NEXT UP . . .

Depending on which course design schedule you are running, one of the following activities follows your discussion on selecting and organizing material:

- A break
- Video examples
- Individual or small group exercise

### Break

If you have scheduled a break, remember to tell them exactly how long they have and exactly when to be back.

## Demonstration: Video Examples

**LEARNING OBJECTIVE:** To illustrate the selection and organization of material based on audience wants and needs

**TIME:** 10–20 minutes

**MATERIALS:** VCR, monitor, videotape of examples

*Facilitator: Video examples are a fun way to illustrate your points. You may be able to get some tapes from in-house presentations at your company, but be careful about using tapes of individuals in your organization as "bad" examples. Or tape speeches from educational TV or political candidates. The only way you can get this wrong is if your clips are too long.*

Show a video and then ask for discussion on what the participants saw that illustrates the discussion about the communication model. Don't be shy about talking over the video to call their attention to things you want them to see.

## Exercise: The Elevator Presentation

(This is an individual exercise that works best for a small class of no more than twelve participants.)

**LEARNING OBJECTIVE:** The purpose of the exercise at this point in the program is twofold:

1. To reinforce what you have discussed so far
2. To get your participants up and speaking, thus introducing the platform skill and feedback sections yet to come

**TIME:** 30–45 minutes preparation time; 2 minutes per person for presentations

**MATERIALS:**
Audience Analysis Worksheet
Outline Worksheet
Presentation Evaluation
Stopwatch or watch with a second hand
Video camera and tapes (optional)

**SCENARIO:** The speaker finds himself or herself on an elevator with a target audience, such as a manager or client. In less than two minutes, the speaker must either introduce himself or herself or offer an update on a project. In both cases, the speaker has been hoping for this opportunity and has already prepared (the Audience Analysis and Outline Worksheets).

*Facilitator: Hand out copies of the worksheets, and give your participants about thirty minutes to prepare. They should complete the Audience Analysis Worksheet and the Outline Worksheet and then review their preparation with the checklist on the Presentation Evaluation in their Handout Packets. Your copy is at the end of this chapter.*

After thirty minutes, ask participants to sign up in the order they want to present. Someone always wants to go first. Ask for a volunteer to keep time, and instruct the timer to wave at the speaker at ninety seconds and say "Thank you; your time is up" at two minutes. Instruct speakers that if they are cut off, they are allowed to finish their sentence, but they may not start another thought. Speakers are to introduce their presentations with information about their target audience and their objective. Start the clock when they start the actual presentation. For more effective role playing, ask another participant to stand in as the manager or client on the elevator (but not to get into a debate with the speaker).

You may choose to videotape these presentations. I rarely videotape short presentations by inexperienced speakers who had short preparation time; they tend to be intimidated by the process and humiliated by the results. I prefer to build confidence by focusing on positive aspects of the presentation, and an individual who views his or her own tape tends only to see the weak points. So if you insist on videotaping, give the tape to the participant to take home. Do not show it in class.

For positive feedback, ask participants to list speakers' names on a sheet of paper and to note positive aspects of the speech and issues that need work. Never use the terms "good" and "bad." Instead, say "good" and "needs work."

Debriefing: At the end of the presentations, ask these questions:

- Overall, what did you see that you liked?
- What did someone else do that you wish you had done?
  (You will get mostly comments on platform skills, so you will have to ask more specific questions about content and organization.)
- How could you tell when the speaker really knew the target audience? Give me an example of such a presentation.
- Which attention-grabbers did you like best? Why?
- Who had the most specific and personal benefit for the target audience?
- Did you hear any good examples of summaries? Action steps? Final statements?

When you have exhausted their input (and don't be disappointed if this doesn't take long), you are ready for the next steps: visual aids, platform skills, and feedback.

## Exercise: The Budget Request

(This small group exercise works best with a larger class of more than twelve participants.)

**LEARNING OBJECTIVE:** The purpose of the exercise at this point in the program is twofold:

1. To reinforce what you have discussed so far
2. To get your participants up and speaking, thus introducing the platform skill and feedback sections yet to come

**TIME:** 30 minutes preparation time; 2 minutes per person for presentations

**MATERIALS:**
Audience Analysis Worksheet
Outline Worksheet
Presentation Evaluation
Blank transparencies
Colored transparency pens
Stopwatch or watch with a second hand
Video camera and tapes (optional)

**INSTRUCTIONS TO FACILITATOR:** Divide participants into small groups of two to three people, depending on the size of the group and the amount of time you have. Count off around the room to avoid groups of people who are already sitting together. If there are more than two people in a group, instruct the group to designate a speaker. Don't worry about this part—they always negotiate well among themselves! With only two people, give them a choice of one or both of them speaking.

Walk around the room, and ask participants to give you a little change. Some people will give a penny; a few get in the spirit and offer up several coins. Ask one participant to count them, and write the total on the board or flip chart, adding several zeros. The purpose of the presentation, therefore, is to convince some decision-making group in the organization how to spend the $237,000 (you can make it $237 million, if you want to!).

Give them blank transparencies and colored transparency pens, just to see what kind of visual aids they come up with. You could get some great examples for your discussion on visual aids later in the day. Hand out copies of the worksheets, and give your participants about thirty minutes to prepare. They should complete the Audience Analysis Worksheet and the Outline Worksheet and then review their preparation with the checklist on the Presentation Evaluation in their handout packets.

After thirty minutes, ask the teams to sign up in the order they want to present. Someone always wants to go first. Ask for a volunteer to keep time and instruct the timer to wave at the speaker at ninety seconds and to say, "Thank you; your time is up" at two minutes. Instruct speakers that if they are cut off, they are allowed to finish their sentence, but they may not start another thought. Speakers are to introduce their presentations with information about their target audience and their objective. Start the clock when they start the actual presentation.

You may choose to videotape these presentations. I rarely videotape short presentations by inexperienced speakers who had short preparation time; they tend to be intimidated by the process and humiliated by the results. I prefer to build confidence by focusing on positive aspects of the presentation, and an individual viewing his or her own tape tends to see only the weak points. So if you insist on videotaping, give the tape to the participant to take home. Do not show it in class.

For positive feedback, ask participants to list speakers' names on a sheet of paper and to note positive aspects of the speech and issues that need work. Never use the terms "good" and "bad." Instead, say "good" and "needs work."

Debriefing: At the end of the presentations, ask these questions:

- Overall, what did you see that you liked?
- What did someone else do that you wish you had done?
  (You will get mostly comments on platform skills, so you will have to ask more specific questions about content and organization.)
- How could you tell when the speaker really knew the target audience? Give me an example of such a presentation.
- Which attention-grabbers did you like best? Why?
- Who had the most specific and personal benefit for the target audience?
- Did you hear any good examples of summaries? Action steps? Final statements?

When you have exhausted their input (and don't be disappointed if this doesn't take long), you are ready for the next steps: visual aids, platform skills, and feedback.

WORKSHEET

# PRESENTATION OUTLINE

## Introduction

- **Attention-grabber.** Based on what I know about my primary audience, what will get his/her/their attention (and also relate to topic and situation)?

___

- **Purpose.** As a result of this message, what do I want my audience *to do?*

___

- Are there any reasons I should be *indirect* with the purpose of this message (including cultural considerations)? If so, how should I temper my expressed goals?

___

- **Agenda.** How am I going to accomplish my objectives; that is, what is my *agenda* for delivering the message?

___

- **Benefit for audience.** What's in it for them, *specifically and personally?*

___

## Conclusion

- **Summary.** Exactly what do I want my audience *to remember* (the essence of my main points)?

___

___

- **Specific action.** Exactly what do I want my audience *to do?*

___

- **Strong final statement.** What is the last thought I want to leave with them?

___

## Body

Choose from these common options:

1. Chronological order for simple, ordered instructions or reports
2. Problem (3 parts) and solution (1 part) for audience with low knowledge
3. Problem (1 part) and solution (3 parts) for audience with high knowledge

   (Note: Your solution should include potential risks.)
4. Current situation and proposed situation (3/1 or 1/3, based on audience knowledge)
5. Inductive format (general to specific) or deductive format (specific to general)
6. Pros and cons (or compare and contrast) for simple analyses or evaluations
7. Decision-making format for complex issues
8. Bad news format for information they do not want to hear
9. STARR format for situation, task, action, result, and recommendations

- Point One: ______________________________

  Support Material (such as statistics or examples):

  ______________________________
- Point Two: ______________________________

  Support Material: ______________________________
- Point Three: ______________________________

  Support Material: ______________________________
- Point Four: ______________________________

  Support Material: ______________________________

WORKSHEET

# PRESENTATION OUTLINE EXAMPLE

***(Note and disclaimer: This hypothetical example was based on the Audience Analysis Worksheet Example in Chapter Five and developed as a class exercise.)***

Speaker: BigMag Sales Manager

## Introduction

- **Attention-grabber.** Based on what I know about my primary audience, what will get their attention (and also relate to topic and situation)?

  *Here's a look into your future: $$$$$$ (unique opportunity for job advancement and additional income)*

- **Purpose.** As a result of this message, what do I want my audience *to do?*

  *Understand the details of the new partnership between BigMag and HugeCorp*

- Are there any reasons I should be *indirect* with the purpose of this message (including cultural considerations)? If so, how should I temper my expressed goals?

  *no*

- **Agenda.** How am I going to accomplish my objectives; that is, what is my *agenda* for delivering the message?

  *Describe the deal (current situation) and highlight opportunities (proposed situation)*

- **Benefit for audience.** What's in it for them, *specifically and personally?*

  *Increased job satisfaction and financial gain*

## Conclusion

- **Summary.** Exactly what do I want my audience *to remember* (the essence of my main points)?

  *The joint venture will increase both the size of the company and the opportunities for you. As the company profits, so will you.*

- **Specific action.** Exactly what do I want my audience *to do?*

  *Embrace the joint venture as a positive and exciting opportunity.*

- **Strong final statement.** What is the *last thought* I want to leave with them?

  *BigMag + Huge Corp = $$$$$ for YOU!!*

## Body

- **Point One:** *Details of the BigMag/HugeCorp deal (current situation)*

  Support Material (such as statistics or examples):

  *Net worth will be $5 billion*
  *Annual sales will double*
  *Market development opportunities will increase*

- **Point Two:** *Highlight opportunities*

  Support Material:

  *More readers, market appeal (more opportunities for sales) Higher stock price, profit (more opportunities for income, benefits) Better image (more opportunities to be proud of your company)*

**WORKSHEET**

# PRESENTATION EVALUATION

SPEAKER:

TOPIC:

SPEAKER'S TARGET AUDIENCE:

EVALUATOR:

Directions for the speaker: Evaluate yourself on each point before you present.
Directions for the evaluator: Evaluate the speaker on each point.

| | Good! | Needs work |
|---|---|---|
| **CONTENT** | | |
| Relevant material for audience's knowledge level | | |
| Acknowledgement of audience's wants and concerns | | |
| Sufficient depth in support material | | |
| Interesting examples for audience and situation | | |
| Appropriate visual aids | | |
| **ORGANIZATION** | | |
| Grabs audience's attention | | |
| States clear agenda | | |
| Includes benefit in introduction | | |
| Follows clear organizational plan | | |
| Summarizes essence of main points | | |
| Asks for clear action in conclusion | | |
| Closes with strong final statement | | |
| **DELIVERY** | | |
| Moves comfortably and gestures naturally | | |
| Looks at each member of the audience | | |
| Speaks conversationally and enthusiastically | | |
| Handles visual aids effectively | | |

Overall comments:

Finally, would you hire this person or buy this product or support this proposal?

# Match the Visuals to the Words

To be effective, visual aids must be appropriate, clear, consistent, and dynamic. They do not, however, require an advanced degree in Presentation Software to prepare, and you do not need extensive knowledge in computer technology to teach preparation of visual aids.

Your purpose in this section of the training class is to teach four critical elements for visual aid design and use, not how to actually use PowerPoint or some other presentation software. If you happen to be technologically proficient, you certainly can answer their questions or demonstrate techniques in your own presentation, but your students can take a computer class to learn the mechanics. The four elements—appropriateness, clarity, consistency, and dynamism—are important to all forms of visual aids, and the rules apply at all levels of proficiency.

I suggest that you present an overview of the following material based on the knowledge level of the participants. Then show examples of a variety of slides, and ask participants what is right or wrong on the slides. Refer to "Guidelines for Visual Aids" in their handout packet (Part Four) for detailed reminders.

---

*Facilitator: An exercise with the "Before" and "After" of four slides follows this chapter.*

---

## Lecture: Guidelines for Visual Aids

**TIME:** 15–20 minutes

**MATERIALS:** Guidelines for Visual Aids
Transparency 14, "Match the Visuals to the Words"

Visual aids serve several important purposes. They:

- Provide an outline for your audience so they know where you've been and where you're going.
- Provide an outline for you so you don't have to manage notes.
- Support your oral message with visual images to increase what your audience remembers.
- Support your words with numbers and graphs to increase what your audience comprehends.

*Facilitator: Display Transparency 14, "Match the Visuals to the Words."*

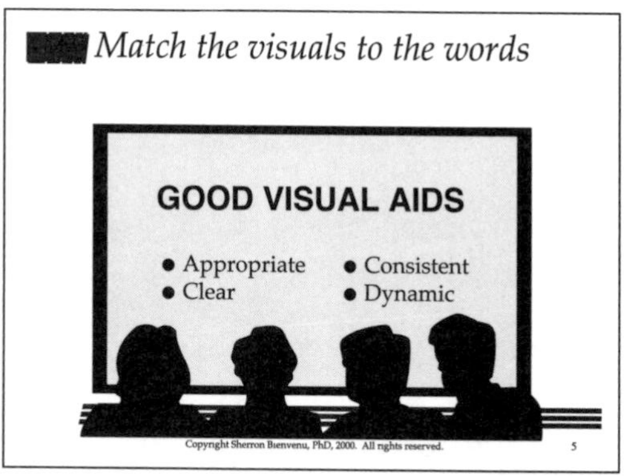


Effective visual aids contain four elements: They are appropriate, clear, consistent, and dynamic. They do not have to be complicated or difficult. If you follow these guidelines, preparing visual aids will be enjoyable, and they will serve all their intended purposes.

## Good Visual Aids Are Appropriate

Your visual aids must be appropriate in terms of type and overall design concept.

**Appropriate type.** To select the appropriate type of visual aids, refer again to your Audience Analysis Worksheet. Look for clues that will help you make decisions about colors, illustrations, even choice of words. Pay attention to the expectations about visual aids in your company, based on its corporate culture. Then meet or exceed these expectations. Evaluate the actual venue in which you will be speaking. Check its lighting, room size, and shape. As a basic rule, the bigger the group, the larger and more formal your visual aids. Your handout (also Exhibit 7.1) lists your options with some of the advantages and disadvantages of each.

HANDOUT

# PRESENTATION VISUAL AID OPTIONS

**Presentation Visual Aid Options with Advantages and Disadvantages of Each**

| *Option* | *Advantages* | *Disadvantages* |
|---|---|---|
| Models, objects | Offer realism<br>Provide hands-on experience<br>Are appropriate for all cultures | Cannot be seen by large groups<br>Detract from speaker |
| Write-on boards, Flip charts, Write-on transparencies | May be generated by audience<br>Create casual atmosphere<br>Appear spontaneous | Indicate lack of preparation<br>Take time during presentation<br>Require good handwriting<br>Are not appropriate for formal cultures |
| Prepared flipcharts | Transport anywhere | Cannot be seen by large groups<br>Are not appropriate for formal cultures |
| Handouts | Add note-taking capabilities<br>Are appropriate for all cultures | Distract from speaker |
| Computer-generated overhead transparencies | Appear professional<br>Indicate preparation<br>Work in lighted room<br>Require only overhead projector<br>Are appropriate for all cultures | Require back-up bulbs |
| Photographic slides | Show vibrant colors | Require darkened room<br>Preclude returning to an earlier point |
| Video cassettes | Show movement<br>Provide variety | Require video cassette player and monitor large enough for audience to see<br>Are expensive to produce |
| Computer-generated slides presented via computer | Appear professional<br>Indicate technical expertise | May require semi-darkened room<br>Require Liquid Crystal Display (LCD) panel, computer, and overhead projector<br>Technically difficult to trouble-shoot |
| Multimedia productions | Create high-tech atmosphere<br>Appear most impressive of all options | Require complex, advanced computer hardware and software for preparation and presentation<br>Distract from speaker<br>Could overwhelm or intimidate less sophisticated audiences or cultures |

*Facilitator: Use the Exhibit 7.1 chart as backup information rather than reviewing the pros and cons in class.*

Remember that *you* are the most important visual element of your presentation, so your audience must be able to see you. Therefore, try to avoid *any option* that requires you to turn off the room lights completely such as photographic slides and some computer-generated slideshows.

**Appropriate design concept.** Always start the preparation of your visual aids by reviewing your analysis of your situation, your audience, and your purpose. Use the details you gathered to make your basic choices of templates, fonts, clip-art styles, colors, and especially words.

If the situation is somber, select serious colors and avoid cartoon clip art. If the audience is multicultural, select easily recognized words and illustrations. If your purpose is motivational, consider themes such as stars, flags, or other icons associated with success. Be creative, but be certain that your overall design is suitable for the occasion, your audience, and your purpose.

## Good Visual Aids Are Clear

Your visual aids will be clear—that is, they will make sense to your audience—if they follow the outline of your speech and if they succinctly present that outline.

**Follow your outline.** Refer to your Outline Worksheet, and start your preparation by designing one slide for each idea. For example, a basic presentation might have the following slides:

1. Title
2. Attention-grabber
3. Purpose
4. Agenda (road map)
5. Benefit for audience
6. Point #1
7. Support or example for point #1
8. Point #2
9. Support or example for point #2
10. Point #3
11. Support or example for point #3
12. Summary (may be repeat of agenda)
13. Action step
14. Final statement

**Keep it simple.** Limit your slides based on the desired length of your speech. Figure on an average of one slide per minute. (Therefore, the speech for the above example would be approximately fourteen minutes.) Then try to limit your material to five lines of copy on each slide. Use no more than seven points for maximum retention. Fewer is better.

## Good Visual Aids Are Consistent

Your slides should be consistent in terms of background, font, structure, capitalization, spacing, and illustrations.

**Background.** Presentation software allows you to select a template for the entire presentation. The more illustrations you plan to use, the simpler your template should be. Choose a style that symbolizes your message or that shows respect for your target audience.

High contrast between background and text provides excellent visibility in a lighted room. Cool, dark colors (blue, purple, black) appear to move away from the audience, and warm, light colors (yellow, white) appear to move toward the audience. Therefore, your audience will be more comfortable looking at visual aids with dark backgrounds and light letters. You might try colors that complement your company logo or that reflect the country or culture of your audience.

**Font.** Your fonts should be consistent in terms of size and type.

All titles should be the same size of the same font, and all body copy should be the same size of the same font. For computer-generated transparencies and slides, I suggest a *minimum* size of 28 pt. for body copy and 36 pt. for titles in most standard fonts. Title fonts should be easily recognized as larger.

There are two basic types of fonts: serif (the letters stand on small platforms) and sans serif. Serif is traditional and easier to read. Sans serif looks more contemporary. Titles and body copy may be different from each other, so you might select a sans serif font for your titles (for dramatic effect) and a serif font for your body copy (for easy reading).
Examples of serif:

Bookman Old Style

Garamond

Times New Roman

Examples of sans serif:

Arial

Univers

Comic Sans

**Structure.** When using bullets on slides, the points should be "parallel"—the grammar should be the same. For example: "Analyze the environment,

Consider the options, Select information" (each clause begins with a verb). Or: "Media, Source, Timing" (each item is a noun). Or: "Overall goal, Specific purpose, Hidden agenda" (each phrase begins with an adjective).

**Capitalization.** Capitalize sparingly. A mixture of uppercase and lowercase letters creates a more natural, easy-to-read visual. You may print your titles in all capital letters, although you may find that a title in all uppercase takes up too much space. Capitalize only proper nouns and the *first letter* of the first word in each bullet point of body copy. Don't capitalize the first letter of every word; everything will look like a title.

**Spacing.** Decisions about consistency in spacing affect your titles, your body copy, and your bullet points.

Your titles should be in the same spot on each slide (such as centered or flush left or right), although you might need two spacing designs, one for one-line titles and one for two-line titles. (If you are using PowerPoint, start by making a decision on single-line titles in your Slide Master, then adjust for two-line titles. Check for consistency by looking at your work on the Slide Sorter.)

Start your body copy at the same spot on each slide. (Again, in PowerPoint, set this up on the Slide Master, then select View Guides to maintain consistency.) You might have a second starting spot for your slides with two-line titles.

The space between your bullets should be consistent as well. Avoid the urge to spread bullets out if you only have two or three. (Use that extra space for a great illustration.) The space between bullets should be about one-and-a-half times the size of the bullet font. A wrapped bullet point remains single-spaced.

*Facilitator: Refer to the lecture slides provided with this book for examples.*

**Illustrations.** Graphs and clip art should be similar in size and type. For example, don't mix cartoon-character clip art with realistic-looking clip art. If you choose photographs, try to use them throughout your presentation. Check your presentation on your Slide Sorter View (in PowerPoint) to be sure your illustrations are about the same size.

You do have several options of where you place your illustrations on your slide. Let the picture and the amount of space you have be your guide. For example, a slide with three long bullets would look good with a wide illustration at the bottom. A vertical illustration that faces right (the picture should always face into the slide to focus your audience's attention on the words) would work on the left side with bullets on the right side.

## Good Visual Aids Are Dynamic

Select powerful words, provocative pictures, impressive charts, and exciting technology.

**Powerful words.** Use action verbs and descriptive adjectives. Don't be shy about using your thesaurus to find exactly the right word, then checking your dictionary to confirm the exact meaning. Be sure your choices are appropriate for your audience's vocabulary.

**Provocative pictures.** The time you invest in finding just the right picture will result in a memorable presentation. Clip-art CDs are inexpensive, scanners are reasonably priced or available at your company, and the Internet is a free treasure chest of incredible pictures, so there is no reason to rely solely on the clip art that comes with your presentation software.

**Impressive graphs.** Illustrations should give your audience the idea, not the detail. Save detailed data for handouts. Select the type of chart based on the relationship you want to show. Exhibit 7.2 illustrates examples of charts. But remember: Simplify, simplify, simplify. After you have designed your chart, edit for clarity and succinctness. A common mistake is to put so much information on a chart that the audience doesn't know where to look. The less material on a slide, the better your audience will retain it.

**Exciting technology.** Technology is wonderful—under three conditions:

1. It works.
2. The speaker knows how to work it.
3. It truly enhances the presentation.

One of the worst things that can happen to a speaker is for the technology to fail. So be sure to test your equipment in advance. Confirm that the computer has enough memory to run your slide show or that the overhead projector bulb is bright enough. Be prepared with whatever extra bulbs, batteries, cords, etc., that you might need.

You will lose credibility even before you start speaking if you don't know how to operate your equipment. If you are using a PowerPoint slide show, rehearse the transitions. Too many speakers are surprised by unexpected sounds or flying bullets. Even something as simple as consistently crooked transparencies can annoy an audience past the point of listening to you. (Hint: Tape a ruler across the top of your projector, then simply slide your transparency frames up against the ruler. You won't even have to look down, and your transparencies will be straight.)

When asked why they added certain "bells and whistles" to their visual aids, too many speakers answer, "Because I could." Not the right answer. Remember that the purpose of visual aids is to support your oral message by helping the audience understand and remember what you say. If they are more impressed by the technology than by your message, you may not accomplish the objectives of your presentation.

HANDOUT

# EXAMPLES OF CHARTS AND THE USAGE OF EACH

## Examples of Charts and the Usage of Each

| *Type of chart* | *Example* | *Use* |
|---|---|---|
| **Pie** | 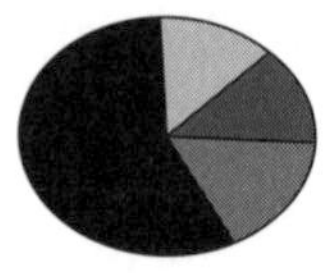 | Component comparisons |
| **Bar** | 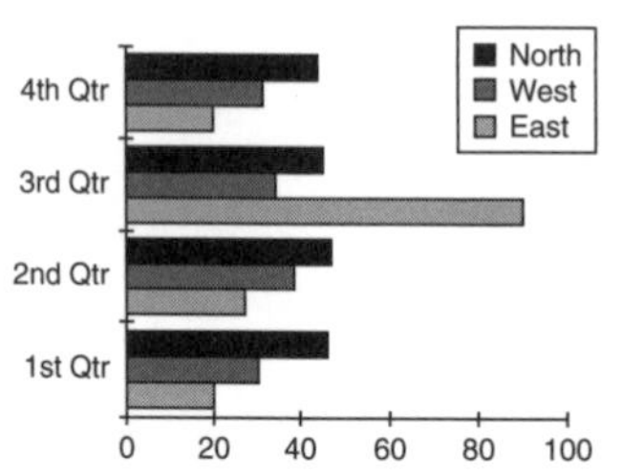  | Ranked comparisons |
| **Column** | 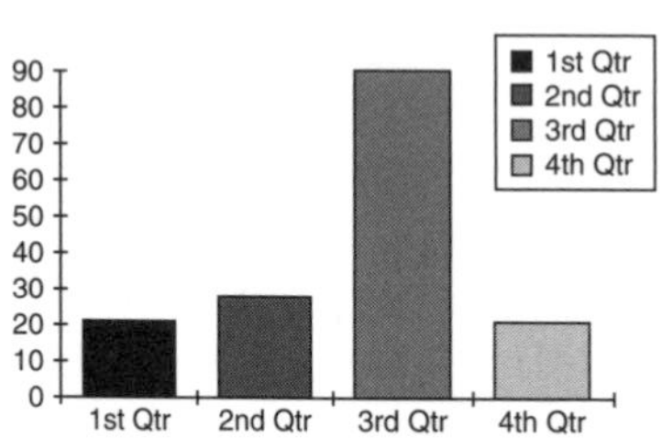  | Variation over time |
| **Line** | 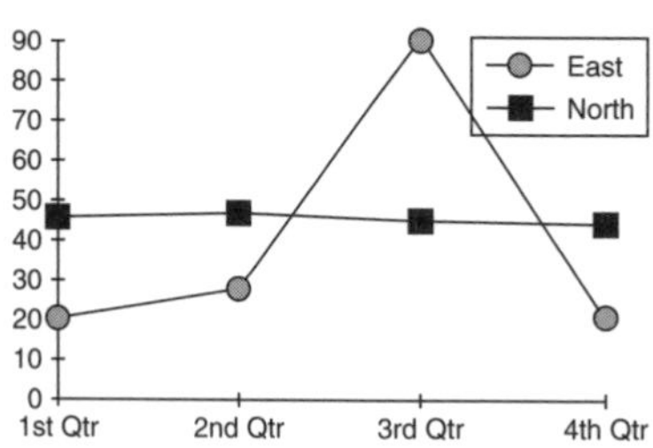  | Variation comparison over time |

## Exercise: Visual Aid Assessment

**LEARNING OBJECTIVE:** To illustrate and reinforce principles of visual design

**TIME:** 10–20 minutes

**MATERIALS NEEDED:**
Transparency Example 7.1
Transparency Example 7.2
Transparency Example 7.3
Transparency Example 7.4
Transparency Example 7.5
Transparency Example 7.6
Transparency Example 7.7
Transparency Example 7.8
Other examples of your choosing

**INSTRUCTIONS TO FACILITATOR:** Create transparencies from the masters at the end of this chapter. Then copy the Notes Page View pages for your notes. Project the "Before" slides, and ask participants for their impressions. Point out the design issues that they miss. Then project the corresponding "After" slides. Have fun. Designing visual aids is an art, not a science, so expect your participants to disagree on what they find most appealing. You should, however, reinforce the basic issues in the Guidelines.

*Facilitator: After the exercise, turn off the projector.*

## MY STORY

*Facilitator: Once again, I suggest that you reinforce what you are teaching with examples. Add an example here to summarize the importance of effective visual aids. You are welcome to use mine until you have some of your own. Then close this section with the material in "Remember."*

### Select Dynamic Illustrations

One of my regular clients, a former Navy pilot in business development with a defense contractor, was preparing a briefing for a Navy rear admiral. The purpose of the presentation was to explain the capabilities of a new airplane. The draft version of the slide show contained too many charts with too many numbers and words.

We decided to try a slide with only an illustration of the airplane on its mission that was communicating with a variety of satellites, ships, and other airplanes. It looked much more interesting than words and numbers, so we created another scenario on a second slide. My client, who was an excellent and knowledgeable speaker, would simply show the pictures and explain the scenarios. He liked the idea but was not sure how this nontraditional concept of presentation—neither words nor numbers on the slides—would be received.

On the day of the briefing, the admiral listened passively until the scenarios were presented. After the second one, he interrupted with "Wait!" My client thought he must have made a mistake with his creative approach until the admiral asked, "Do you have another scenario of another mission?"

This one incident had more impact on the preparation of presentations at that company than hours of training could have. Success is a powerful training tool.

## Be Prepared to Troubleshoot

The Hotel Loftleidir in Reykjavik, Iceland, has a perfectly designed auditorium with state-of-the-art equipment and a full-time technician. It is a trainer's dream. Ten minutes before my Success Strategies for Women Seminar was to begin, with fifty professional women waiting to enter the room, I connected my laptop to check how my slides looked when projected on the huge screen. To my dismay, my beautiful dark blue background appeared black, and the lighter blue lines that pulsed across the screen when the slide changed did not show at all.

There was a time when I would have just used whatever I got. However, I had created my own slides and knew how to use the software program. In seconds, I was able to adjust the color, thus achieving the effect that I had planned.

The lesson, of course, is to learn to make your own slides. When you are giving the presentation, it's your credibility—yours alone—that will suffer if you have problems with your visual aids.

---

## Lecture: Summary of "Match the Visuals to the Words"

**TIME:** 2 minutes

Visual aids provide an outline for both you and your audience, and they enhance the meaning of your presentation so that your audience better understands and remembers what you say. To be effective, your visual aids must be appropriate, clear, consistent, and dynamic. But always keep in mind that they are *aids;* they should never distract from you or your message. They should only enhance your presentation.

**HANDOUT**

## VISUAL AID EXAMPLES

EFFECTIVE PRODUCT ORGANIZATION

- product types are logically arranged
- individual products in the right area
- safe and attractive physical plant

What's wrong:

- Title font and body copy are the same size—Arial 36 pt. (body copy is too large).
- Clip art is too small, looks out of the picture, and doesn't enhance the message.
- First letter of first word of bullet points is not capitalized.
- Copy is not parallel.
- Space between lines appears to be same both *within* the bullets and *between* the bullets (space should be greater between bullets).

(continued)

HANDOUT

# EFFECTIVE PRODUCT ORGANIZATION

- Logically arranged product types
- Strategically placed individual products
- Safe and attractive physical plant

What's right:

- Title font is larger than body copy font (Title font is Arial 44 pt.; body copy is Times New Roman 32 pt.).
- Clip art is appropriate size, focuses the audience's attention toward the body copy, and enhances the message.
- Body copy is parallel with stronger words (such as "strategic" instead of "right place").
- More space appears between the bullets than within the bullets; i.e., there is more space between "products" and "safe and attractive" than there is between "strategically" and "safe."

(continued)

HANDOUT

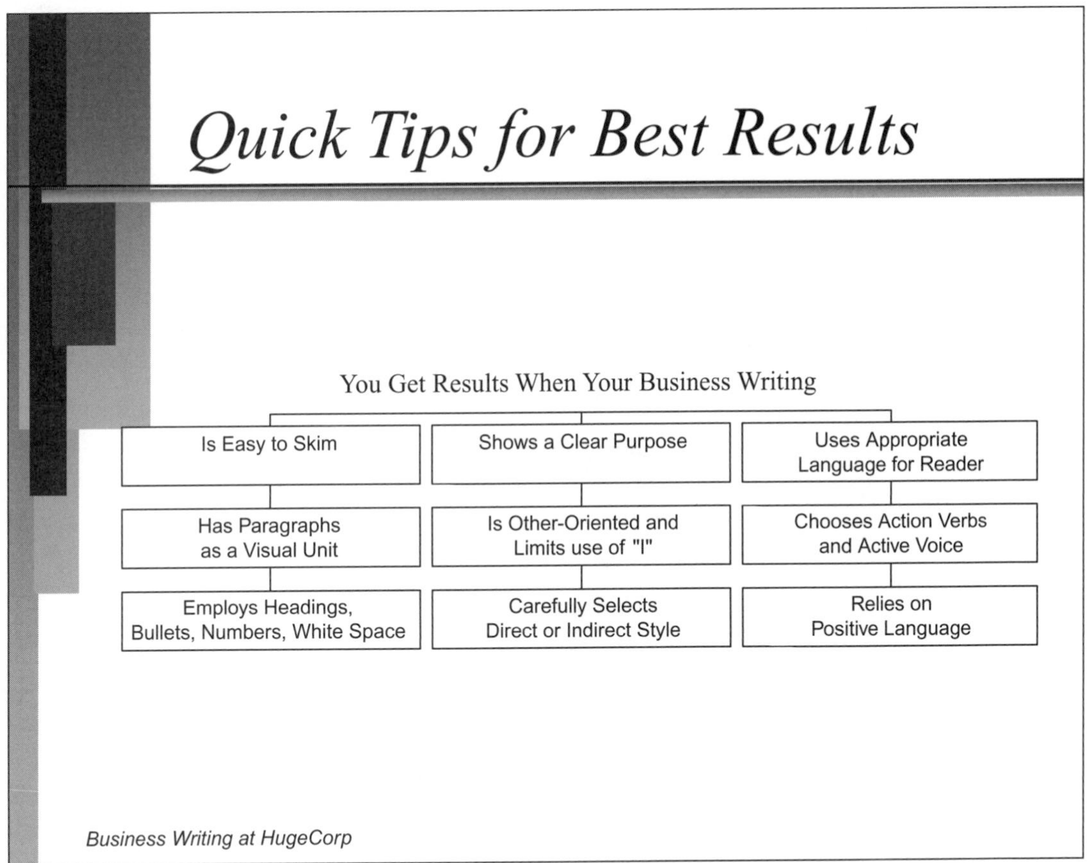


What's wrong:

- Reader does not know where to look: too many boxes, too many points (many of which are redundant), too many words.
- Body copy is too small (Arial 20 pt. in boxes).
- The first letter of every word is capitalized; therefore, every phrase reads like a title.
- Design is clever but distracting.
- Body copy is not parallel (all boxes start with a verb except "carefully").
- Some verbs are weak ("has" and "is").

(continued)

What's right:

- Six bullets summarize the nine previous points (but the wrapped copy in the third bullet should line up with the copy on the first line).
- Copy is parallel and easy to read.
- Template and clip art enhance the message.
- The title font is Times New Roman 44 pt. (serif), and the body copy is Arial 28 pt. (sans serif).

Reminder about fonts: There are two basic types of fonts: serif (the letters stand on small platforms) and sans serif. Serif is traditional and easier to read. Sans serif looks more contemporary. Titles and body copy may be different from each other, so you might select a sans serif font for your titles (for dramatic effect) and a serif font for your body copy (for easy reading).

(continued)

## EXAMPLE: BUYING CALLS, POTENTIAL PROFIT AND LOSS

- **Buy a call option for $2, giving you the right to buy a share of stock for $70**
- **However, your option expires in May**
- **If the stock price goes above $72 before May, you can exercise your option and make a profit**
- **The higher the stock price (above $72), the greater your profit**
- **If the stock price does not go above $72, your loss is limited to $2**

What's wrong:

- Too many words; all the audience will see is a paragraph.
- Bullet points are not parallel.
- Coin template is clever since the presentation is about money, but coins indicate a tiny profit.
- This font is Garamond (26 pt. in title and 18 pt. in body).

(continued)

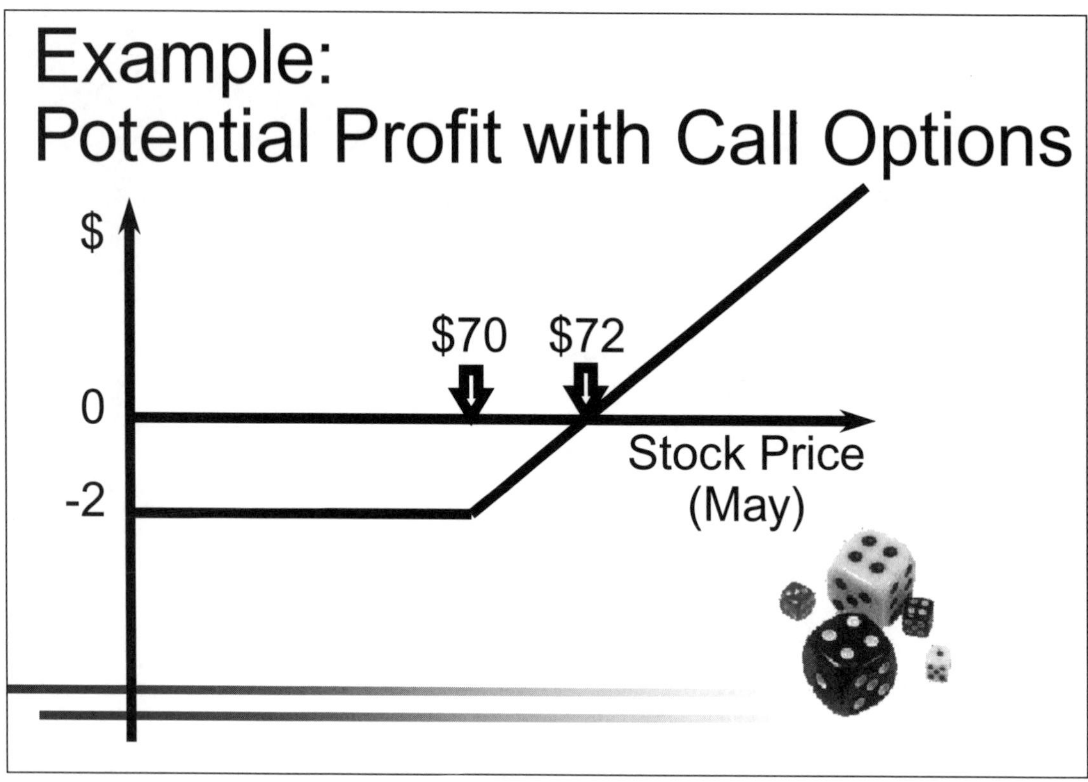


What's right:

- Graph is a clean illustration of the material in Example 7.5.

*Note: An option is to prepare a handout for your audience by giving them detailed material (such as the information in Example 7.5) in the format shown on this page: Smart Notes: When a speaker has too much material for a slide, one option is to put a simple version on the slide for the presentation, and then put all the support material into the notes. If the speaker gives a handout, the handout can be Notes Pages rather than the 3-to-a-page version (such as in the handout package with this book).*

- Template suggests risk and provides better contrast.
- Arial font (44 pt. in title and 28 pt. on graph) is modern and easy to read.

(continued)

HANDOUT

# Summary of C-130J Improvements

- The C-130J Takes Off Faster
- The C-130J Flies Higher and Farther with the Same Load
- The C-130J Cruises at a Higher Speed for a Longer Range with a Heavier Load
- The C-130J is Less Expensive to Maintain Over the Life of the Aircraft

What's wrong:

- Too much body copy, some of which is redundant.
- Too many capitalized words (only the first letter of each bullet point and proper names should be capitalized).
- Title copy and body copy are both serif fonts, but they are *different* serif fonts (Bookman Old Style 42 pt. and Times New Roman 24 pt., which is also too small).
- Photo is pretty and flying into the slide, but it is too small.

(continued)

What's right:

- This slide summarizes and offers a strong final statement.
- The picture is a dramatic enhancement.
- Title font and footer font are the same (Perpetua 58 pt. and 32 pt.). Italics suggest movement.
- Sans serif body copy (Universe 28 pt.) is strong and modern.
- The simple black line around slide frames the message.

# Deliver Your Presentation

Comments during the Presentation Challenge Exercise, video clips, and individual or group presentations will have set you up for your discussion on Step Four of the Strategic Communication Model: Deliver your message. The most important points for you to make and reinforce are:

- Each speaker is different.
- Individuality makes each speaker successful as a presenter.

I usually begin this section by posing this question: "Let's assume, for a moment, that a speech is perfectly organized and comprises perfectly focused information based on the needs of the target audience. What platform skills will make a speaker good?"

You will get responses about energy, eye contact, confidence, etc. You can comment on these particular skills based on the information below, or you can list them on a board or flip chart and refer to them as you move through your discussion.

There is a plethora of information available on platform skills—too much to digest—which is why I focus on four basic areas. Based on what you have learned about your participants, you can adjust your material to better reflect their specific concerns. For example, executives may not need information on speech anxiety at all, but entry-level employees may need demonstrations and practice sessions on the anxiety-reducing exercises.

Use the following material (which contains additional notes to you in italics) as the basis of your lecture on platform skills.

## Lecture: Platform Skills

TIME: 20–25 minutes

MATERIALS: Transparency 15, "Deliver Your Message"
Transparency 16, "Polish Your Verbal Skills"
Transparency 17, "Polish Your Nonverbal Skills"
Transparency 18, "Know Your Material"
Transparency 19, "Express Confidence"
Transparency 20, "Be Yourself"

Now that you have that perfectly organized outline of perfectly focused material, let's discuss the fourth step in the Strategic Communication Model: Deliver your message.

*Facilitator: Display Transparency 15, "Deliver Your Message."*

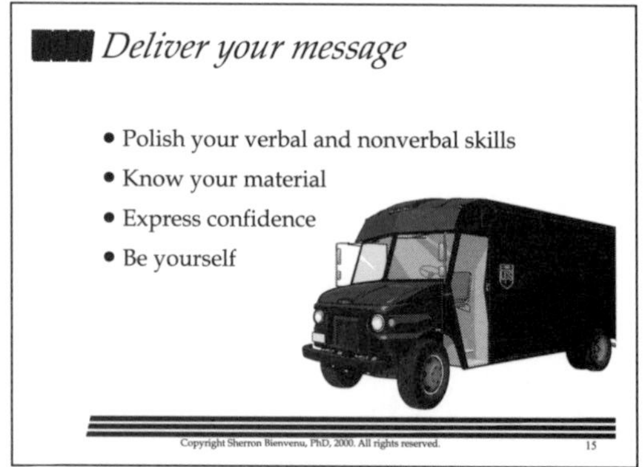


We're going to concentrate on the following key elements of your presentation style:

- Polishing your skills
- Knowing your material
- Expressing confidence
- Being yourself

The decisions you make about your communication style over the course of your career should be determined by your specific audiences and the culture of your industry. There are, however, some generic guidelines for success, a few tricks, and some common mistakes to avoid.

*Facilitator: Since the lists of verbal and nonverbal skills are long, you can use this an example of how to group topics so they are more easily remembered.*

## Verbal Skills

*Facilitator: Display Transparency 16, "Polish Your Verbal Skills."*

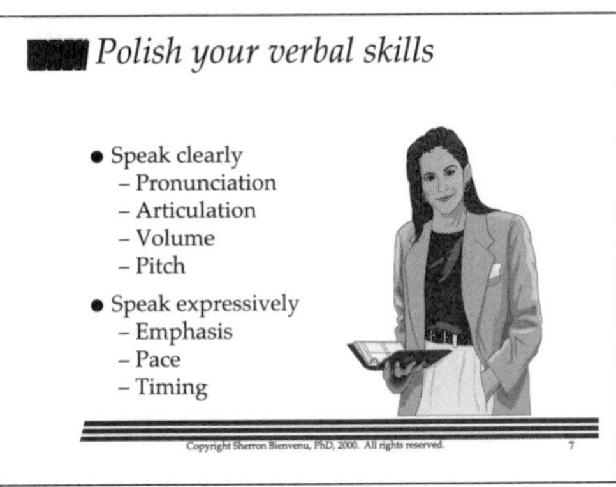


Your verbal skills include the technical aspects of the way you use your voice—pronunciation, articulation, volume, and pitch—and the dramatic aspects—emphasis, pace, and timing. Good verbal skills enable you to speak clearly and expressively.

**Speak clearly.** Concentrate on improving your pronunciation, articulation, volume, and pitch so that your audience can easily and comfortably hear and understand your words.

Pronounce words correctly. Just use one "bid-ness" for "business" or "pitcher" for "picture," and you will lose credibility with your audience.

*Facilitator: This section of the workshop can be very entertaining for your participants. Ask for examples of frequently mispronounced words and repeat them. Have fun demonstrating common mistakes that speakers make, thus establishing that no one is perfect, everyone can improve, and most problems are easy to fix. Your attitude will set a less intimidating mood for later in the workshop when participants give and receive individual, specific feedback.*

Articulate your words. Say all the letters in all the syllables of every word. Don't relax into "lemme" for "let me" or "gonna" for "going to."

*Facilitator: Ask for more examples and elaborate on them.*

Speak loudly enough for the back row to hear you, but be careful about being too loud for the front row. One myth is that if you speak quietly, an audience will lean in to hear you. The truth is that if you speak softly, your audience is likely to go to sleep. If you have trouble speaking loudly enough, avoid the old-fashioned advice about opening your mouth wider. You'll feel like the wide-mouthed frog. Instead, simply concentrate on talking with the people in the back row as if they were the decision makers. This focus will help you increase your volume.

Find your lowest pitch and try to stay in that range most of the time. Here's the trick: Lie flat on your back (at home, please!) and relax. Breath from your diaphragm without moving your shoulders (this is easier to learn while lying down than while standing up). Then read out loud. The pitch you hear is your natural pitch. Try to maintain it when you stand up. Then practice finding the same sound when you are standing up by simply relaxing and breathing from your diaphragm. Do not, however, maintain this pitch monotonously. The idea is to speak naturally, just a little lower and with more resonance.

*Facilitator: To demonstrate, take a couple of slow, deep breaths from your diaphragm. Then speak with a lower, more resonant voice.*

**Speak expressively.** Work to perfect your emphasis, pace, and timing so that your audience can easily understand the meaning of your words.

When you outline your presentation and practice your delivery, determine which words are the most important, and then underline or highlight those words in your notes. When you speak, you can emphasize words by changes in volume, pitch, pace, or timing.

*Facilitator: Demonstrate by reading the following sentence in a flat monotone: "We need more vacation time." Now, read it again, first emphasizing "we," then "need," then "more," and then "vacation time." Then show the difference in "Don't! Stop!" and "Don't stop!"*

Many speakers get feedback that indicates they talk too fast. But trying to "slow down" may seem awkward. A better alternative is to identify material that is new, difficult, unusual, or particularly important for the audience and focus on presenting that information at a slower pace. Then return to your comfortable, normal, faster pace. Again, you may want to highlight this important information on your outline.

One of the most dramatic effects a speaker can learn to use is timing. The pause can be a powerful emphasis tool. There are many places a pause can enhance your presentation:

- After you walk to the front of the room but before you begin speaking
- Before you make an important point ("This is the bottom line": . . . pause . . .)
- After you make an important point ("Our profits would be in the millions." . . . pause . . .)
- When you ask a question (pausing may feel awkward and so most speakers don't wait long enough)
- As a transition between main points ("That sums up the problem." . . . pause . . . "We are looking at several solutions.")
- After your final statement and before "thank you"

The pause always refocuses the audience's attention, so learn to use it often and wisely.

## Nonverbal Skills

*Facilitator: Display Transparency 17, "Polish Your Nonverbal Skills."*

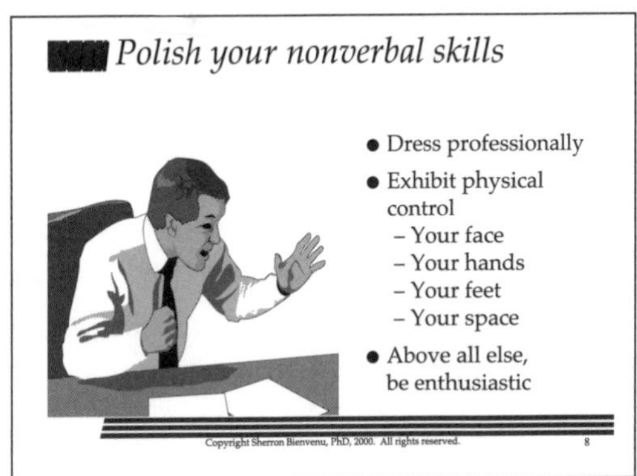


Your nonverbal skills include two basic areas: how you look and how you move. Obviously, you should take your cues from your target audience and your organization, but some fundamental nonverbal abilities are essential.

**Dress professionally.** This goes without saying. The one rule, however, is that if you are not sure how to dress, you are better off being overdressed than underdressed.

Most importantly, don't wear anything that is distracting. Men should not wear ties with odd patterns or belt buckles with unusual designs. If they are short, stout, or gesture broadly, they should not wear a double-breasted jacket. Women should not wear anything that moves or makes noise (dangling earrings, charm bracelets, etc.). They should not wear stockings or shoes that are lighter than their skirts or pants, unless the shoes and stockings are skin-toned and neutral. They should not select bright nail polish or unusual make-up colors. If you ever find yourself tugging at anything, then you know what to fix the next time. (For example, if your hair falls in your face, either cut it or fasten it back.)

**Exhibit physical control.** Your audience should believe that everything you are doing with your face, your hands, your feet, and the space around you is a result of a conscious decision.

Start your presentation with a smile. It relaxes both you and your audience. Look for other places in your speech when a smile would be appropriate as well. The rest of the time, use facial expressions to enhance the emotions you are communicating with your message. And don't forget to look at your audience. Look at each individual as if you were having a conversation with that person. If you do not make eye contact with your audience, you will lose their attention.

The two mistakes with hand gestures that speakers make are contriving hand movements and leaving their hands in the wrong place for too long. Contrived movements make you look silly; inappropriate hand placements create a variety of distractions.

Some trainers actually teach their students to create visual pictures of their words. Just let your hands do what they naturally do; hands hanging casually at your side look much more comfortable than unnatural gestures.

*Facilitator: Use an example such as, "We could see money flying out the window," or "Our hearts broke as the stock crashed." Accompany your verbal example with exaggerated hand gestures like flapping arms for flying or clutching a broken heart.*

The rules for where you can actually put your hands have relaxed somewhat. Speech teachers used to have clear lists of "do" and "don't" positions. Now, for example, it's perfectly all right to put a hand in your pocket if you are not making your most serious point. But here are some bad movements to avoid:

- If you put your hands in your pockets, be sure they fit, and don't wiggle your fingers.
- Don't cross your arms (conveys defensiveness) or put your hands on your hips (looks angry or aggressive).
- Men should not "fig leaf."
- If your hands shake when you begin to speak, inconspicuously hold on to the lectern or clasp your hands behind your back, but don't leave them in either place for the duration of your speech.
- Be careful about repetitive hand movement. If you think you are using the same "chopping" gesture all the way through your presentations, videotape yourself and then watch the tape on fast-forward. Not only will you catch the repetitious motion, you will probably cure yourself of doing it!

Keep your weight on both feet. Again, this sounds obvious, but speakers tend to forget that the audience can see their feet. They will cross them, bounce, and rock back and forth, all of which can be terribly distracting. If you concentrate on keeping the weight on the balls of your feet, you will be balanced and ready to move when you want to.

The space at the front of your room is yours, so use it to enhance your presentation. The rule about moving around is: "Walk, or stand still." When you are standing still, stand completely still. Do not dance with your feet, your knees, or your shoulders. When you walk, do it for a reason. Changing your position in the room can show a natural break in the content of your talk, reattract the audience's attention, give them a chance to adjust their own physical position, emphasize a point, or create a transition.

*Facilitator: Ask participants for examples of anything else they can think of that speakers do that is annoying. They may realize that everyone commits some annoying behaviors, which leads to your next point: enthusiasm.*

Remember one overriding delivery skill as you continually perfect the appropriate communication skills that will enable you to be more and more effective with your target audiences: enthusiasm. Your audience will forgive you if you walk too much or not enough, if you sometimes talk too fast, if you look down more than you should, if you forget to smile, etc. They will *never* forgive you—and you will never achieve your objectives—if you are not enthusiastic. You must show sincere enthusiasm for them, for their needs, and for your objectives. Above all else, you must master the skill of expressing enthusiasm. Your audience will appreciate this.

## Know Your Material

*Facilitator: Display Transparency 18, "Know Your Material."*

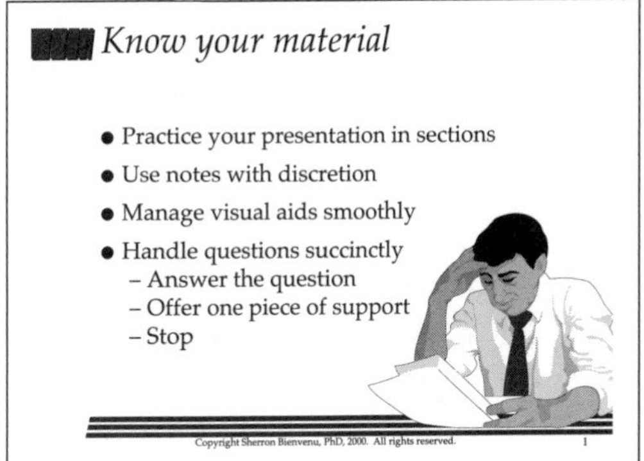


The second key element of your presentation style is how you demonstrate to your audience that you know your material. Four points are critical to this process:

- How you practice your material
- How you use your notes
- How you manage your visual aids
- How you answer questions

**Practicing Your Material.** You have already prepared an excellent outline, and your main points are supported by interesting examples, so a lot of your work is done. There are, however, four things that you may want to rehearse: your introduction, stories, transitions between main points, and conclusion.

The best way to practice is to work on one small section at a time, such as the introduction or the transition from your introduction to your first main point. Don't write your speech word-for-word. If you memorize it, you will sound like you are reciting rather than having a conversation with your audience. Instead, practice each section until you are comfortable and fluent. Even if it comes out a little different during the actual presentation, your speech will still sound natural and spontaneous.

Ideally, you should have someone videotape you. I certainly suggest this for very important presentations, especially if you are a beginner. If video taping is not possible, the second best place to work is in front of a large mirror so you can see your nonverbal behavior while you are going over the words. Do not practice with *only* an audio tape recorder. A flat verbal recording without the enhancement of your nonverbal skills is not sufficient feedback.

*Facilitator: Ask participants if they have ever practiced these rehearsal techniques and what were the results. Often people will comment about their voices sounding funny when they hear it on tape. Explain again the importance of seeing the presentation as well as hearing it, since so much of communication is nonverbal.*

**Using Notes.** If possible, avoid using notes altogether during your presentation and just use your visuals. Well-prepared visual aids provide a useful set of notes for your presentation. You should be familiar enough with your topic to rely almost entirely on the outline on your slides, that you have designed from your Outline Worksheet. However, even the most prepared and knowledgeable speaker presents material that is new or complex to the point that the material on the visual aids is not enough. And in some presentation situations, visual aids are not appropriate, such as a speaker introduction or a luncheon speech. In that case, I suggest putting notes on a 5 ξ 8 card so that you can carry them with you if you move away from the podium.

The biggest preparation mistake a speaker can make is to write a speech down word for word. If you write it, the chances are that you will read it. Reading a manuscript, no matter how well written, will negate the positive effects of all your other work on your presentation. You will appear unprepared and unprofessional. You will severely diminish your chances for success. The only exceptions to this may be in diplomacy or when presenting a carefully worded press release where a misstatement could create legal difficulties.

**Managing Your Visual Aids.** Your objective with your visual aids is to convince your audience that you are the one in control. Your visual aids should not appear to be managing you (like the dog who "walks" the owner).

First, learn to work your equipment. Know, for example, how to get back to your previous slide. Be prepared to use either the keyboard or a cordless mouse. Check that bulbs in your overhead projector are bright enough and that markers for your flipchart are fresh.

When you are presenting, focus on your audience, not on your visual aids. Avoid facing the screen, and avoid either reading the slides or talking to them, the latter of which looks really silly. You may turn and gesture toward the screen to draw your audience's attention to a bullet point or illustration, but immediately turn your face and body back toward your audience.

Almost every culture reads from left to right, and after we blink or look down, we automatically look to the left first. Therefore, you should stand to the audience's left of your visual aids, so their focus is first on you and then on your visual aids. Remember, you are most important; your visual aids are just that—aids to support you and your message.

**Handling Questions.** The two issues regarding questions are when to take them and how to answer them. Planning the "when" part makes the "how" part easier.

**When to answer questions.** Some speakers feel that they lose control of the situation when the Q&A section starts, so they avoid it as long as possible in hopes that time will run out. I advise a different strategy.

First, tell your audience when you are going to take questions during your presentation. If you are comfortable with interruptions, encourage them, but be aware that you are likely to be interrupted with a question about something that you are about to cover. When that happens, you either have to jump ahead in your organization (not the best solution) or tell the questioner that you will address the material soon.

Most speakers are better off announcing that they will take questions at the end of each section or at the end of their presentation. This avoids the problem of having the speech organization thrown off and gives them the opportunity to answer most of the questions that would have come up.

Second, decide exactly when you will ask for questions at the end. You have two choices: before your summary or after your summary. Either place is fine, depending on your personal preference and style. However, do not wait until after your final statement to ask for questions. Invariably, the last question you receive will be the one that is awkward for you to answer, and that will then be your final impression on your audience. Instead, tell your audience something like this: "I'll take one last question and then I have a final thought to leave with you."

Third, review your notes about your final statement from your Outline Worksheet. If you take questions after your summary, you might want to briefly summarize again, perhaps enhancing that summary with issues you addressed in your Q&A. But always leave the audience with a strong, carefully rehearsed final word.

**How to answer questions.** Entire books have been written on strategies for answering questions. The basic plan, however, comprises three simple steps:

1. Answer the question.
2. Offer one piece of support.
3. Stop.

You don't need to go on and on, which is the most common mistake that speakers make when answering questions.

The second most common mistake is stumbling over questions that you don't know the answers to. It's perfectly fine—actually, it's preferred—to just say, "I don't know." But always follow up with a comment about finding the answer and getting back to the person who asked the question.

## Express Confidence

*Facilitator: Display Transparency 19, "Express Confidence".*

A good presenter is like a duck—calm and serene on the surface and paddling like crazy underneath. There is no way to be truly confident unless you live in an ideal world. However, you can look and sound confident about your argument, your organization, yourself, and the inevitable "disaster" by remembering some points about confidence:

**Confidence in Your Argument.** If you have completed your homework, including thoroughly analyzing your audience and selecting material based on the needs of that audience, you should have confidence in your argument. If you have taken any shortcuts, then you might have excluded vital information. The time you invest in preparation always pays off.

**Confidence in Your Organization.** Organizations, like families, are not perfect. But also like families, you don't want to air your company's "dirty laundry" in public. Find places in your presentation to demonstrate your belief in your company, whether you are speaking to an internal audience or to clients. Expressing confidence in your organization builds trust in you.

**Confidence in Yourself.** No matter how confident you are about your argument, you are likely to experience speaker anxiety. "Stage fright" is normal; it's your body's adrenaline kicking in, which provides extra energy. In fact, I worry more about speakers who say they are not nervous at all, since an audience might perceive that relaxed attitude as lack of enthusiasm.

Everyone's nerves show in a different place. Here are some tricks for combatting these common nervous conditions:

- **Racing heart.** If you have time on the morning of your presentation, plan a workout or a run. If your time is limited, find some way to get your heart rate up. Even if you are in a hotel room, you can do situps, pushups, and squats. If you have back-to-back meetings before your presentation, go out and walk around the building a couple of times to burn off excess energy and take advantage of the extra oxygen.

- **Dry mouth.** Chew your tongue. I know this sounds disgusting, but chewing your tongue creates saliva and helps dry mouth. Don't do it where people can see you—you'll look like a cow.
- **High or weak voice.** Since most people would like their voices to sound stronger or lower, let's take a moment and try an exercise.

---

## Exercise: Breathing

TIME: 3 minutes

LEARNING OBJECTIVE: Demonstration of an easy trick for quick voice improvement.

INSTRUCTIONS TO FACILITATOR: Demonstrate these techniques as you describe them. Ask your trainees to participate.

1. Your lowest natural pitch is supported by good breath control from your diaphragm. So, as you are waiting to speak, first concentrate on deep breathing.
2. Concentrate on moving your belt buckle in and out when you inhale and exhale. Don't move your shoulders when you breathe deeply; such heaving motions tighten the muscles around the throat and exacerbate the problem.
3. Borrow a relaxation strategy from yoga: Inhale on two counts, hold for two counts, then exhale for four counts.
4. If you have a table in front of you, lean forward and put your elbows on the table. No one will see you breathing.

This exercise offers several benefits:

- You will relax, because you are concentrating on counting your breathing rather than stressing about your speech
- Your pitch will drop, because you have relaxed the muscles in your neck and chest, and you are supporting your voice from your diaphragm
- You will be more centered and focused psychologically, because you have taken control of the physical anxiety.

- **Shaky hands.** While you are waiting to speak and while no one is looking, make hard fists and then stretch out your hands several times to increase blood flow and therefore control. However, if something is shaking, don't show it to the audience! Avoid holding up your hands. In most cases, your hands will stop shaking when you get involved with your presentation.

- **General insecurity.** This is my best all-purpose solution: Stand up straight. Nothing conveys personal confidence better than good posture. The extra benefits are that you look more attractive and you can breathe better. Lift your chest, pull your shoulders back and down, and raise your head. Face your audience squarely with your body, and look your audience in the eye. Smile. You're ready to go.

## Confidence in Disasters

Why did I put this last? Because no matter how prepared you are and how confident you appear, something unexpected is going to happen. Your computer could crash, you could fall on the way to the podium, or something could fly out of your hand and hit your boss in the head. Most likely, however, the computer will only be unplugged, you will only trip (but not fall), and the flying object will miss human targets. The less you make out of the incident, the less the audience will notice.

But never ignore the problem. For example, if you drop a pencil, pick it up. If you trip over a chair, make a small joke about coordination not being in your job description, and move the chair out of the way. If you skip a bullet on a slide, say something like, "But before we move on, let's go back to the second point." If it doesn't appear to bother you, it will not distract your audience.

*Facilitator: Ask for horror stories your participants have seen or experienced. How were they handled? What else could have been done? You'll get some great examples for future training.*

## Be Yourself

*Facilitator: Display Transparency 20, "Be Yourself."*

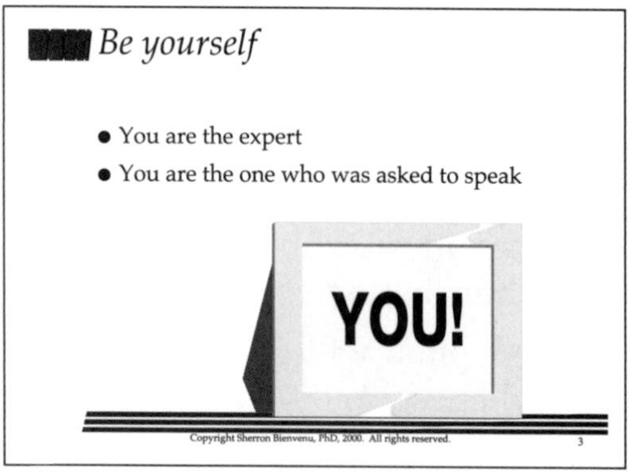


Most people are comfortable one-on-one but believe that they must become someone different when they address a group. They have seen effective speakers and try to emulate their excellent platform skills. But even though it is valuable (and recommended!) to learn delivery techniques from other people, you should not try to become someone else. It is you who were asked to speak, not some other person. You might have to talk louder or gesture more broadly, but whatever makes you effective one-on-one should also apply to the louder or broader you. Allow your personality to be reflected in all your communication. In brief, be comfortable as yourself. You are as good as anyone, and you are probably a lot better with the topic you've prepared.

*Facilitator: Turn off projector.*

## MY STORY

*Facilitator: As you finish this step of the Strategic Communication Model on delivering a presentation, share your own experiences with speakers who have impressed you. Use positive and negative examples to make your points. You might also sprinkle these examples throughout your lecture. "My Story" should help you remember some stories of your own, or you can use the following examples.*

I've trained thousands of people in platform skills, and most of those individuals delivered presentations to me two or three times as part of the training. I guess I've seen just about everything that anyone could possibly do in front of an audience.

Rather than sharing just one story, I'd like to share a list of some winning and losing behaviors.

### Winners

I'd like to tell you about some people who taught me what it takes to be a great presenter. These are some of the people from whom I learned:

- **Ruth Alexander.** When I first saw "Miss A" speak, I was a freshman at Centenary College. She had the most expressive hands I had ever seen (and have yet to see) and a voice that painted pictures. Every word and every gesture had meaning; she wasted nothing. I wanted to be just like her. I wanted to emotionally move an audience the way she did.
- **Joe McCann, PhD.** When I first saw Joe speak at a meeting and manage fourteen people with fourteen agendas, I wanted to be just like him. He was the calmest person I had ever seen, and he was in complete control of himself and of that meeting. He had the ability to think quickly on his feet, but when he spoke, he spoke slowly and with authority. His movements were slow and controlled, almost like a cat stalking prey. I went home and stood in front of a mirror and tried to look and sound like Joe.
- **Annette Shelby, PhD.** When I first saw Annette present at an Association of Business Communication national conference, I wanted to be just like her in every way. I had no female role models at my university that

compared to her. Her research topic was interesting and provocative, her organization was specific and focused, she looked professionally elegant from head to toe, and (this is what really got to me) she never looked at the projector when she changed her transparencies, yet they were always straight. I was transfixed by her perfection.

- **Paul Timm, PhD.** When I first saw Paul speak, he was standing in front of a large group of serious colleagues who had "heard it all." He opened his presentation with a cartoon. Everyone loved it. And when he talked to the group, we all felt like he was talking with each of us individually. He was natural, and his audience was charmed. I wanted to be just like him. I wanted my audiences to like me as much as his audiences liked him.

## Losers

I learned from these next people, too, but there will be no names. These were some of the worst situations I have ever seen. I hope none of us ever falls into these traps.

- The corporate CEO who put his head down and read a forty-five-minute after-dinner speech in a mumbling monotone. The material may have been good, but no one cared. The only people who were still awake when it was over were those who worked directly for him. He is no longer the company's spokesperson.
- The self-proclaimed communication consultant who arrived at her speaking engagement wearing a short red dress that was at least a size too small. She took her high heel shoes off and put them back on twelve times during her presentation, thus changing her height twenty-four times. When she prepared her flip chart, she couldn't fit her bullet points on the chart, so she wrote vertically in the margin. She was not invited back.
- The hospital development executive who was too lazy to write down the names of the people to thank at a huge fundraiser and too vain to put on his glasses to read the notes he did bother to make. When he addressed the crowd of 600 people, he forgot to thank the largest donors, thus embarrassing both the organization and the volunteer chairpersons of the event. He is no longer in fund raising.
- The motivational speaker who relaxed into a "canned" presentation for every audience with no analysis of individual groups. When beginning a speech to a civic group, he looked around the room, saw numerous plaques on the walls, and opened with compliments about the group's achievements. He never connected with his audience. The room was also used by the Boy Scouts, and they won all the awards. The civic group wanted a motivational speaker because they were not motivated to go out and do anything that would win awards.

## Lecture: Summary of "Deliver Your Presentation"

**TIME:** 2 minutes

Improvement of delivery skills is a life-long project. Polish your verbal and nonverbal skills to develop a style that meets your audience's expectations and is comfortable in their corporate culture. Speak clearly and expressively. Dress professionally. Exhibit control with appropriate facial expressions, hand gestures, and body movement. Above all else, be enthusiastic.

Prove that you know your material by thoroughly rehearsing in advance. Be comfortable with your notes and your visual aids. Be prepared to answer questions. Never, never read.

Express confidence in your material, based on your preparation, and in your company, based on your experience. Exhibit confidence in yourself, even in the face of adversity.

Most of all, be yourself. That's whom the audience came to see. You are the most important part of your message, and your unique personality is your most valuable platform skill.

# Evaluate Feedback

Your discussion of giving and receiving feedback, the final step of the Strategic Communication Model, should begin by explaining how improvement in presentation skills is based on realistically evaluating feedback from target audiences and trusted colleagues. After discussing the value of feedback, move on to the four parts of teaching the feedback process:

1. How to give feedback
2. How to solicit feedback
3. How to receive feedback
4. How to evaluate yourself: the Credibility Test

Your objective is to train your participants to assess accurately when their communication is "working" and when it is not. Their objective is to modify the areas that are less effective. This is tough to do and sometimes even tougher to teach. Many people consider their communication skills to be a part of their personality, and they take communication skills feedback more personally than feedback on, say, accounting skills.

An additional objective for you as the facilitator is to establish an environment in your workshop that fosters constructive feedback—one in which participants feel "safe" giving and receiving feedback. Your guidelines for giving feedback need to be nonthreatening to the recipients, and your examples should reinforce the positive aspects of the process.

Base your discussion on the following material (and, as usual, note the additional comments to you in italics). After the lecture material, we'll talk about the presentation assignments, and I'll offer you some help on what words to say when you give feedback on your presentations in class.

## Lecture: Giving and Receiving Feedback

TIME: 15–20 minutes

MATERIALS: Transparency 21, "Evaluate Feedback"
Transparency 22, "Giving Feedback"
Transparency 23, "Soliciting Feedback"
Transparency 24, "Receiving Feedback"
Transparency 25, "Evaluating Yourself: The Credibility Test"

## Why Feedback?

Being an effective presenter requires an ongoing process of practice and improvement. Yes, you have to get feedback, and no, you won't get any better by presenting over and over in exactly the same way. After a speech, most of us would just like to hear "great job!" and go home. But "great job" doesn't help us improve.

As we move into our discussion of the last step of the Strategic Communication Model (Evaluate Feedback), you might also argue that you've done it all—you've thoroughly analyzed your audience, carefully selected material based on the needs and concerns of that audience, cleverly organized your information, and dynamically presented your message. Why do you need feedback?

The purpose of feedback is to find out if you have met your objectives and to realistically assess the impact of your communication on your audience. You must confirm perception: Did the audience perceive your material the way you intended?

*Facilitator: Display Transparency 21, "Evaluate Feedback."*

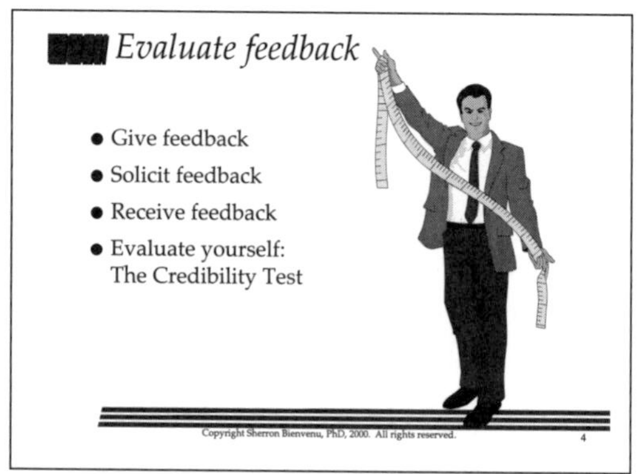


There are four parts to the feedback process:

1. Giving feedback
2. Soliciting feedback
3. Receiving feedback
4. Evaluating yourself with the Credibility Test

*Facilitator: If you are running the longer workshops with individual presentations and peer evaluation, stress the application of this material both in class and on the job. In a shorter, "refresher" workshop for experienced speakers, stress the application in their daily routine as spokespersons for the organization.*

These four parts work best when using clear guidelines. An additional benefit for you is that these guidelines not only will improve your presentation skills but they also apply in other situations that profit from feedback.

## Guidelines for Giving Feedback

*Facilitator: Display Transparency 22, "Giving Feedback."*

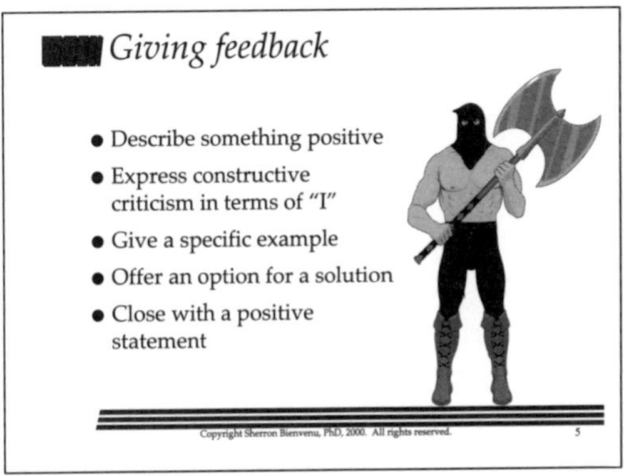


If you only offer positive feedback, you are cheating everyone. The speaker will miss the opportunity to learn from matching your perceptions with his/her intentions. You will miss the opportunity to learn from recognizing your own shortcomings through seeing them in someone else's presentation (sometimes we have to see someone else do something ineffective before we realize that we do it ourselves). The organization will miss the opportunity to improve how ideas are communicated or how products are sold.

Truly useful feedback is that which first recognizes excellence, then points out a need for improvement, and finally offers a suggestion for how to make that improvement without demotivating the speaker. The organization of this feedback message is an application of the bad news pattern:

- Describe something positive first.
- Express constructive criticism in terms of "I" (such as "I needed . . ." or "I didn't understand . . .").
- Give a specific example.
- Offer an option for a solution.
- Close with another positive statement.

For example, you might say something like this: "Your attention-grabber was great! What a terrific story about the improvement in the team *(positive opening)*. However *(transition)*, I didn't understand the explanation of the change in the cost of raw materials *(constructive criticism in terms of "I")*. Maybe a graph or an illustration of some kind would have made it clearer for me *(option for solution)*. Since you tell such good stories, I know you can even make the numbers simple and interesting for us nonnumbers types *(positive, motivating close)*."

With this organizational pattern, both the giver and the receiver tend to be more comfortable with the feedback process. If you are giving feedback, you should be less reticent to offer constructive criticism because you are also recognizing positive aspects. If you are receiving feedback, you should be less defensive about criticism because you are also receiving praise.

## Guidelines for Soliciting Feedback

*Facilitator: Display Transparency 23, "Soliciting Feedback."*

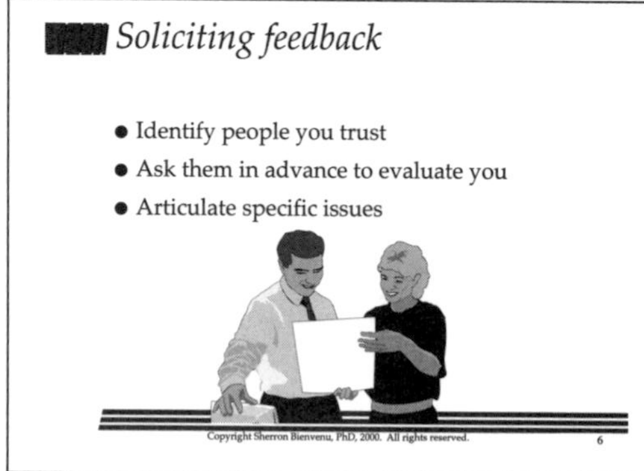


The individual who gives feedback is not the only person responsible for improving communication. As speakers, we also need to ask for feedback.

"So, how'd I do?" however, may not be the best question to ask if you really want thoughtful feedback. You may get "great" and feel better, but you won't get the information you need to learn and grow.

Here are three simple guidelines for soliciting feedback that will help you get better:

- Identify individuals in your audience whom you know and trust.
- Ask them *in advance* to evaluate your presentation.
- Articulate specific issues that you need them to pay attention to.

For example, you might ask a colleague who is not very familiar with your department to assess your description of the need for a new procedure. You could ask someone whose platform skills you admire to watch for specific mannerisms that you could improve. Or you might ask your favorite cynic to look for holes in your argument.

## Guidelines for Receiving Feedback

*Facilitator: Display Transparency 24, "Receiving Feedback."*

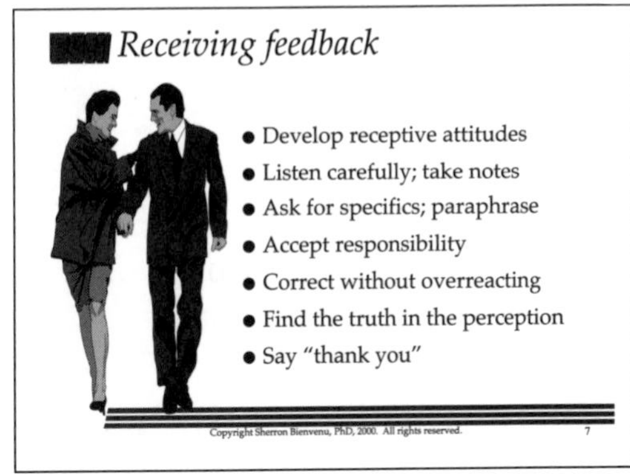


Several extreme behaviors are natural when receiving feedback, such as overreacting ("Fine. If that's how you feel, then I just won't use my hands at all next time!"), disregarding ("Yeah, okay, whatever."), or blaming others ("My assistant gave me the wrong information."). None of these reactions will help you improve. Here are some guidelines for developing positive behaviors:

- **Develop feedback-receptive attitudes.** Nobody likes hearing criticism, but negative feedback can be some of the best information you'll ever get.
- **Listen carefully to comments.** We all have natural tendencies to simply not want to hear someone with whom we disagree, but it is important to hear *everything* you are told.
- **Take notes in detail.** Write down both positives and negatives, noting questions and disagreements.
- **Ask for specific information.** Ask for examples and try the phrase, "Please tell me more." (This is a tough one—we may not want "more" feedback unless it's positive!)
- **Paraphrase to confirm meaning.** Use the reflective technique to gain more information. For example, "This is what I hear you saying. . . ." Your perceptions may not be consistent with your evaluator's intentions. For example, "You are going too fast for me" could refer to the logic in your argument or the rate of your speech.
- **Notice nonverbal messages from your audience.** For example, the person leaning forward is probably more receptive to your message than the person leaning back.
- **Correct in the *direction* of the evaluation.** One tendency is to overreact and to correct to the extreme. A small correction in the right direction is usually more appropriate and more feasible. For example, feedback such as "this makes no sense at all" probably means that your argument needed

more support or your transitions did not connect your ideas. Look for ways to make more "sense" rather than starting over or quitting altogether.

- **Accept responsibility.** Resist the tendency to offer explanations, justification, or apologies for any actions that generate negative feedback. Don't defend yourself or argue with your critics. No one really wants to hear excuses, especially after being asked to give an evaluation, and no excuse facilitates improvement. Remember, you do not have to *accept* all feedback as equally valuable, but you are responsible for determining which is most useful to you. The ultimate accountability for your communication is, after all, yours.
- **Recognize that your audience's perceptions define their reality.** Don't reject comments with which you disagree; there is some truth in practically every comment. Try to find that truth and learn from the knowledge it offers.
- **Say "thank you."** Giving feedback can be as stressful as receiving it. Positively reinforce your evaluator. This will facilitate the future flow of information.

## Guidelines for Evaluating Yourself: The Credibility Test

*Facilitator: Display Transparency 25, "Evaluating Yourself: The Credibility Test."*

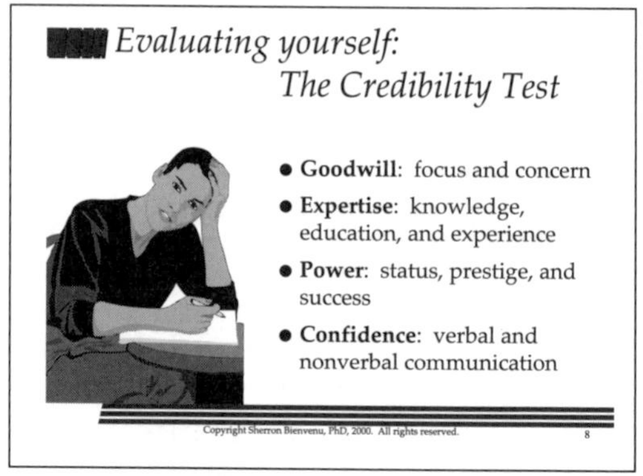


The most important element of your communication strategy is the perception of credibility. If your audience perceives that you are credible—if they believe you, trust you, have confidence in you—you will be persuasive. And if you are persuasive, you will get what you want: You will achieve the objectives of your presentation.

Credibility is the audience's perception of the speaker's characteristics. The only reality is the perception of that audience. Your intention doesn't count; how credible you think you are doesn't count. All that matters is what the audience perceives.

Credibility contains four dimensions: goodwill, expertise, power, and confidence. The Credibility Test is your way of double-checking the decisions you made as you worked through the Strategic Communication Model and prepared your presentation. The Credibility Test is your way of evaluating yourself.

*Facilitator: Ask participants to turn to the Credibility Worksheet in their handout packet. Your copy is at the end of this chapter.*

**Goodwill.** The first dimension of the Credibility Test is goodwill, which is the audience's perception of your focus on and concern for them. In other words, goodwill is your audience's perception of what you think of them. This dimension is about them, not about you. It's their perception of what you think about them—how unique they are, how special they are, how important they are to you or your organization. This one is listed first because if you don't pull it off, you won't have a chance with the other three dimensions.

You will achieve the perception of goodwill from carefully selected information based on your analysis of your situation, audience, and objectives. So obviously, if you haven't thought carefully about the people hearing your presentation, you won't be successful on this dimension of credibility. Review the personal and professional facts, cultural backgrounds, attitudes, and consistent concerns that you noted on your Audience Analysis Worksheet. Also consider what you do outside of work in teams and groups and how those experiences might be transferable examples.

**Expertise.** The second credibility dimension is expertise, which is the audience's perception of your education, knowledge, and experience relevant to your topic. Expertise is your audience's perceptions of the facts about you. Of course, this one requires a balancing act; you don't want to come off as cocky or conceited, but you do want them to think you are smart.

You will achieve the perception of expertise through illustrations that demonstrate your knowledge, education, and experience. It's your chance to share the impressive facts about yourself, relative to your speech topic.

For example, you might include such phrases as:

- "In my twelve years of selling consumer products . . ."
- "The current research on this process suggests . . ."
- "Last week's training class covered that process. Several steps have changed since I first learned about it in my MBA program. . . ." (If you said, "I have training and an MBA, so I think . . . ," you would sound conceited, and therefore you would lose credibility, not gain it.)

**Power.** The third credibility dimension is power, which is the audience's perception of your status, prestige, and success. Power arises from formal position, association with others who have power, authority you have, and accomplishments. Power is your audience's perception of what other people think about you. Keep in mind that an individual's status, prestige, and success may be perceived differently depending on the specific culture of an organization or industry.

You will achieve the perception of power by using material that refers to your rank and illustrates your successes. This is your opportunity to mention any positions, associations, or accomplishments that would illustrate power to this specific audience.

For example, you might be able to make a connection with your audience if you attended the same college, served in the same branch of the military, worked in the same functional area, or belonged to the same organization.

**Confidence.** The final credibility dimension is confidence, which is the audience's perception of how you present yourself—how sure you are of yourself and your message.

You will achieve the perception of confidence through excellent communication skills, which always include doing your homework and preparing messages tailored to your audiences' needs and concerns. Once the material is right, it's easier to feel confident. In addition, people who are perceived as confident are perceived higher on the other three dimensions.

*Facilitator: Turn off projector.*

## Exercise: The Credibility Test

TIME: 10–20 minutes

LEARNING OBJECTIVE: To practice self-evaluation

MATERIALS: Copies of the Credibility Test

INSTRUCTIONS TO FACILITATOR: Since the primary purpose of the Credibility Test is self-evaluation of decisions about material selected for a specific presentation, select this exercise only if you have extra time. Hand out extra copies of the Credibility Test.

INSTRUCTIONS TO PARTICIPANTS: The primary purpose of the Credibility Test is self-evaluation of decisions about material selected for a specific presentation. However, let's practice. For the purpose of this exercise, please consider your direct supervisor. Complete the test by evaluating how your daily communication influences that individual's perception of your credibility. You have ten minutes.

DEBRIEFING: At the end of 10 minutes, ask these questions:

- What did you learn about yourself?
- What are you going to do to correct how you influence perception?

## Lecture: Summary of "Evaluate Feedback"

**TIME:** 1 minute

You will not know how effectively you have communicated with your audience until you have gathered and reviewed feedback. Through careful evaluation of feedback, you will learn if their perceptions matched your intentions. Be conscientious when you give feedback, sincere when you solicit feedback, and gracious when you receive feedback. Be tough on yourself when you take the Credibility Test—your self-evaluation that is your final check before you present. Feedback is your best tool for improvement.

## NEXT UP . . .

Depending on which Course Design schedule you are running, one of the following activities follows your discussion on feedback:

- Summary of the Strategic Communication Model, assignment of four-minute speech for the next half-day, questions, and session take-aways
- Summary, questions, and final take-aways
- Assignment of three-minute speech for afternoon

## Lecture: Summary of the Strategic Communication Model

**TIME:** 1–2 minutes

**MATERIAL:** Transparency 26, "You Will Be Successful"

*Facilitator: If you are finishing the first half-day (or the only half-day), you should summarize the model. Cover the following material as you tell your audience what you want them to remember.*

*Facilitator: Display Transparency 26, "You Will Be Successful."*

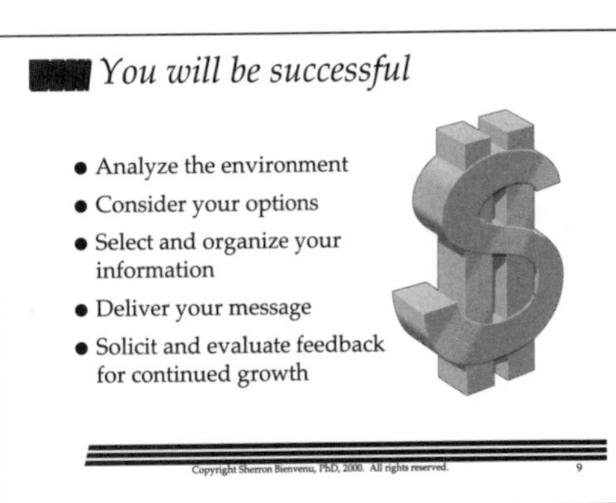


So that's it: The Strategic Communication Model, a clean, five-step, strategic process that will make you more credible and more persuasive when you present (and, as an added benefit, when you write, interview, or interact in teams and groups). Using the Strategic Communication Model will ensure that you appear focused, organized, consistent, and confident. Remember:

- Learn everything you can about the environment: the current situation, your target audiences, and your objectives with each of those audiences.
- Consider your options: Who should send the message, how should the message be sent, and when should the message be sent?
- Use that knowledge to select and organize specific information to meet your objectives with your audiences.
- Deliver your message with a confident, personal style.
- Evaluate feedback for continued growth and success.

Your messages will be focused and confident; you will be perceived as credible, and therefore persuasive; and you will increase your overall effectiveness as a communicator. You will become a great presenter.

*Facilitator: Turn off projector.*

## Questions and Take-Aways

Ask for questions about the model, about any other material you have covered, and about relevant applications in their work environments. Then ask for their "take-aways" (key information they will apply) with questions such as:

- What have we talked about today that will be useful to you?

*Facilitator: As participants respond, elaborate on how "useful" to them will translate into "effective" with audiences. You are looking for comments on each step of the model.*

- How will you prepare your presentations differently as a result of this workshop?
- How will you deliver your presentations differently as a result of this seminar?

*Facilitator: Reinforce the positive effects of these changes.*

- What change will be hard for you to make?

*Facilitator: This is your opportunity to review specific steps of the Strategic Communication Model one more time.*

If you are concluding your program, repeat a brief summary of the model. Then add a final statement such as, "Thank you for your attention over the last few hours. As a result of this seminar, your messages will be more focused, you will be perceived as credible and persuasive, and you will achieve your objectives as great presenters."

## Exercise: Speech Assignments

**LEARNING OBJECTIVE:** Application of all five steps of the Strategic Communication Model

**TIME:** Variable

**MATERIALS NEEDED:**
Audience Analysis Worksheets
Outline Worksheets
Credibility Worksheets
Presentation Evaluations
Blank transparencies and colored pens (if students are preparing their presentations over lunch in the workshop room)
Video camera and tapes

**INSTRUCTIONS FOR PARTICIPANTS:**
These criteria are consistent:

- Select an audience that you give presentations to at work. (You will be presenting to the class, but the class will role-play your target audience.)
- Identify a specific situation and objective for that audience.
- Complete the Audience Analysis, Outline, and Credibility Worksheets.
- Review the Presentation Evaluation as you rehearse.
- Conform to time constraints.

*Facilitator: Review your logistics decisions for preparation and presentation times.*

- For workshops with a second round of speeches, incorporate the feedback from your first presentation.

This criterion is flexible:

- Prepare appropriate visual aids.

*Facilitator: If participants are working over lunch in the training room, give them blank transparencies and colored pens. If they have office time before they present, require better quality visual aids that reflect corporate expectations.*

**INSTRUCTIONS TO FACILITATOR:** Ask participants to sign up in the order they want to present. Ask for a volunteer to keep time and instruct the timer to wave at the speaker when he or she has one minute and to say "Thank you; your time is up" at the end of the allotted time. Instruct speakers that if they are cut off, they are allowed to finish their sentence, but they may not start another thought. Speakers are to introduce their presentations with information about their target audience and their objective. Start the clock when they start the actual presentation.

If you have access to a video camera, you should videotape these presentations. I *never* show participants' tapes in class, but I always insist that they review them in private to compare peer evaluation with their own self-evaluation. A video technician is wonderful, but if none is available, simply ask another participant to insert the video tape and push "record." You don't need fancy camera work.

## But What Do I Really Say?

**INSTRUCTIONS TO FACILITATOR:** Before participants present, hand out copies of the Presentation Evaluation (in their handout packages and at the end of this chapter). You may use the same form for your evaluations or if participants speak more than once over the course of the workshop, you may use the Presentation Evaluation Tracking Form. Since you are simultaneously reviewing your comments from an earlier speech and watching the speaker, you can easily track the speaker's progress.

**INSTRUCTIONS TO PARTICIPANTS:** Make a note about the speaker's target audience, and listen to the presentation as if you were in that audience. The feedback criteria are divided into content, organization, and platform skills. Based on your perception as the target audience, determine whether the speaker does a good job or needs work on each criterion. Remember, you are not helping the speaker improve if you evaluate every criterion as "Good!" In addition, you help yourself if you recognize areas that need work because you may need to work on the same things. When you find an area that needs work—an opportunity for improvement—make a note that will help you remember a specific example to share with the speaker.

**INSTRUCTIONS TO FACILITATOR:** After participants present, lead the class in applauding. This gesture, while perhaps not standard for many workplace speeches, sets a positive tone for feedback. The added bonus is that clapping releases some physical tension for those in the class who are nervous and raises the heart rate for those who are considering a nap.

After the applause, I typically ask two opening questions:

- **To the speaker:** "How did you feel?" (usually followed by "Why?") This gives me a sense of how well speakers think they did overall. If they think they did worse than they really did, focus your feedback on building confidence. If they think they did better than they really did, work to bring their personal assessments in line with reality.

- **To the class:** "What did you like?" This gives me a sense of what impressed the group the most. Class responses usually concern natural, dynamic platform skills, indicating to me that most people would like to be natural and dynamic themselves. After hearing several presentations and my feedback, they start mentioning content and organization specifics.

Then ask the audience questions that cover the points on the Presentation Evaluation, but be careful to ask for specific examples, such as:

- What was it about the material that made it particularly relevant for the audience's knowledge level?
- Where exactly did the speaker acknowledge his/her target audience's concerns?
- Give me an example of an illustration that was particularly meaningful to you as the target audience.
- What was the specific benefit for the audience?
- Show me an example of a hand gesture that you thought was particularly natural.

When you have obtained as many contributions as possible, start your feedback by saying something like, "This is what impressed me." Then go down the list by commenting on the criteria from the Presentation Evaluation. Support your comments with explanations. For example:

- "Your attention-grabber was wonderful because the story centered around saving money, which is what concerns the target audience."
- "The graphs not only were technically impressive; they also made the increases look startling, which is what you wanted to achieve."
- "Your eye contact with the audience made us all feel like you were talking to each of us individually. We are each your new best friend!"

Then, of course, you must tell the speakers what you want them to work on. Don't say, "That was what you did right; now here is what you did wrong." Preface your remarks with a smile and say, "This is what you need to work on." If you have already covered all the positive feedback, you don't have to repeat it here; however, you should conclude your list by reviewing what you particularly liked.

Here are the most typical issues and how I address them:

**Content Feedback.** Most business speakers do a pretty good job with overall content, so you may have to listen very closely and pay careful attention to the speaker's audience analysis to catch the problems here.

- **Telling the audience what they already know.** "Since you were speaking to members of the executive staff, they would already know about the problem. Instead of giving them so much detail, summarize the parts of the problem that would be most affected by your solution."

- **Focusing benefit on themselves, rather than on the audience.** "In your introduction, you stated that managers would have more autonomy as a result of this new operating procedure. However, throughout the speech, you focused on how the company would benefit instead of reinforcing your original benefit to the managers. They are sitting in front of you, and they are the ones who will make or break your idea."
- **Using examples that are not applicable.** "The story about the little old lady at the supermarket was hysterical. The metaphor was wonderful. However, I'm concerned that your audience members don't spend much time at the supermarket and that your meaning might be lost on them. A story about a frequent flyer executive at an airline counter might be more appropriate."
- **Selecting language that is too technical.** "Every day at work, we talk to people who do what we do, so we all talk alike. We use the same jargon, understand the same technical terms, and design acronyms for just about everything. When we talk to people outside our regular circles, however, we often continue to talk the same way, and then we don't understand why they are confused. I know I'm not an engineer, but it would have taken an engineer both *in your department and in your company* to keep up with you when you described your proposed solution. Remember that your audience—and particularly your decision makers—rarely know as much specific information about your job responsibilities as you do. Double-check your material against your Audience Analysis Worksheet to be certain that it matches the knowledge level of your audience."

**Organizational Feedback.** The most common speaker mistakes are in organization; they are also easiest to catch. They are:

- **Skipping the attention grabber.** "It's hard to stand up in front of an audience and not say, 'Good morning; my name is John, and I'm here to talk about the budget.' That sounds like what we hear most of the time. However, if you take a moment to grab your audience's attention first with startling numbers or a great story or a simple question, they will more likely stay focused on the rest of your presentation."
- **Generalizing the benefit.** "The benefit for the audience should be personal and specific. Sometimes the most obvious benefit is for the company, as you stated: 'If we do this, our profits could increase by 10 percent in the next fiscal year.' That's great, and as members of the company, your audience will nod and appear engaged. But what they really want to know is the benefit *for them.* Will this increase translate into more income, more employees, more budget, etc.?"
- **Reviewing the titles of the main points.** "Summarize the essence of the main points. A common mistake is to just mention the titles of the main points, such as, 'I've discussed the problems with the new equipment and

how to solve them.' Instead, tell the audience what you want them to remember about the problem and about the solution."

- **Summarizing only half the speech.** "You did a great job of telling us what you wanted us to remember about the solution, but you should also remind us what the problem is. Restating the essence of the problem supports the need for your solution when you ask for action at the end."
- **Asking for questions at the end.** "If you ask for questions at the very end, you might get a killer question last, and your not-so-impressive answer will be the last words your audience hears. Instead, ask for questions before or after your summary. Tell your audience that you have some closing remarks after their questions, and then be prepared with a dynamic final statement."

**Platform Skills Feedback.** Remind your participants that everyone perceives platform skills differently. For example, enthusiastic gestures might keep one person involved and annoy another person. Some common mistakes:

- **Standing behind the lectern.** "The more time you spend away from the lectern, the more confident you will look. If you must use your notes, at least step back a foot or so to remove the illusion of being 'attached' to the lectern. With each presentation, try to move away more often, especially when you are telling stories or making an important point. If you have good visual aids, use them instead of your notes."
- **Dancing in one spot.** "The rule is to walk or stand still. When you are standing in one place, you should really stand still. It's fine to gesture, of course, but don't 'dance' with your feet, knees, hips, or shoulders. Keep the weight on the balls of your feet, and stand tall."
- **Looking at the screen.** "Speakers are sometimes captivated by their projected slides and seem to forget about their audience. It's fine to refer to your slides with a gesture or a glance, but quickly return your focus to your audience."
- **Talking too fast.** "Many speakers talk too fast and argue, 'But I'm a Yankee; we all talk fast!' However, meeting your objectives requires that your audience understand what you say. No one expects you to totally alter your speech patterns, but when you need your audience to completely understand information that is new, difficult, or especially important, concentrate on pronouncing every syllable in every word and *slo-ow do-own!* Then you can resume your usual pace. In addition to increasing your audience's understanding, the change in pace will refocus its attention on you and your message."
- **Reading.** "There were two of you speaking today: Alice #1 was looking down and reading her material. It was wonderful material—beautifully written—but we could have read it ourselves. Alice #2 was looking at us and talking to us. We cared a lot about Alice #2 and her message, even

though sometimes it was not as 'perfect' as the material Alice #1 read to us. Watch your tape and notice how effective Alice #2 is with her audience. Then next time you prepare a presentation, don't write everything down. Find places to just talk to your audience. Increase that 'talking time' with each presentation. We'd like to see Alice #2 all the time."

*Facilitator: This is a tough one. It's difficult to get readers to be spontaneous. Usually, however, there is some point at which they do not read. Look for that time and use it in your feedback.*

## MY STORY

It's hard enough to give negative feedback in a class where participants anticipate evaluation. As a trainer, however, you might also face situations where you need to give feedback to people (often company executives) who did not ask for your opinion about their presentations. The effectiveness of such feedback may depend on the timing of your message.

In my position as communication consultant to a regional real estate development company, I was invited to attend the annual stockholders meeting. The main purpose was for me to hear the corporate strategy as it was being presented to the stockholders and to get a better sense of the overall culture of the organization.

Knowing I would be asked for my impressions, I took notes on everything, including how the room was set up, how the guests were greeted, and how the executives presented their information. Overall, it was a successful event. However, the CEO *read* his speech.

I was surprised because he was a brilliant man—confident, successful, articulate, attractive, sincere—but much of what made him so effective was lost as he read his manuscript. The message was carefully prepared, but his audience received none of the benefit of his dynamic personality. They just heard words.

I knew that it was my responsibility to give him constructive criticism about his presentation. But he didn't ask me, so I didn't offer the information. I waited.

Months later, I was included in a planning session for an annual conference of marketing managers from all the regional offices. The CEO was preparing a talk to open the conference that would explain his perspectives on building a successful company and motivate the participants to share his vision. As he briefed us on his draft, he spoke from his heart. His face, his eyes, his hands, his voice all enthusiastically enhanced his message. He was captivating.

When he finished, he asked me what I thought. At last I had the opportunity I had been waiting for. I commented on the relevance of the message and the clarity of the strategy. And then I said something like this: "Most importantly, I believed you, and I believed *in* you. When you deliver this message, do it exactly the way you did just now: Look at your audience, talk to your audience, be yourself. If you write this down and read it, you'll lose 40 percent of your effectiveness."

He looked at me without saying a word. I wondered if he knew that I had "estimated" the 40 percent part, but I had used a number because he was a "numbers" person. After a few long moments, he went on with the meeting. I wondered if my comments had made any impact.

At the end of the meeting, he summarized by listing each person's responsibilities and concluded with his own, the last of which was ". . . and I will work on my speech until I can deliver it without losing that 40 percent."

The day of the meeting, he walked to the front of the room with notes in his hand, put them on a table, and *talked* to his audience. He was incredible. He not only set an open, honest tone for the meeting, he also established a model for communication within the company.

I realize, of course, that this CEO knew he was more effective when he talked than when he read. But I also realize that even the smartest, most successful people need some feedback. As a trainer, it is your responsibility to identify how presentations can be improved, even if you have to wait months to offer your suggestions.

## REMEMBER

As tough as feedback may be to give, it is only by receiving *thorough* and *explicit* feedback that your trainees learn and improve. Be open to feedback yourself. Be a role model for the skills you teach. Then recognize every opportunity for improvements that you can share with the individuals in your class as they demonstrate their skills. Explain the needed changes, demonstrate the techniques to implement the changes, and motivate participants to incorporate those techniques into their preparation and delivery processes. Finally, enthusiastically recognize improvement and reinforce the personal and specific benefit derived from the investment. It's a long way from just "Great job!"

WORKSHEET

# PRESENTER CREDIBILITY

***Goodwill:***
**The audience's perception of my focus on them and my concern for them.**

What do I do to show my target audience that I care about them?

______________________________________________

______________________________________________

What do I do with my friends that illustrates teamwork?

______________________________________________

***Expertise:***
**The audience's perception of my knowledge, education, and experience.**

What knowledge, education, and experience do I have that might impress my audience?

______________________________________________

______________________________________________

This is something that I have accomplished that I am really proud of:

______________________________________________

***Power:***
**The audience's perception of my status, prestige, and power.**

What is my rank in the organization, and how might this impress my audience?

______________________________________________

______________________________________________

What awards or recognitions have I received that might impress my audience?

______________________________________________

Here is an example of my personal power (my ability to control my own environment):

______________________________________________________________

______________________________________________________________

______________________________________________________________

Here is an example of my interpersonal power (my ability to influence other people):

______________________________________________________________

______________________________________________________________

______________________________________________________________

Here is an example of my corporate power (my ability to mobilize resources):

______________________________________________________________

______________________________________________________________

______________________________________________________________

Here is an example of relationships that give me "power by association":

______________________________________________________________

______________________________________________________________

______________________________________________________________

***Confidence:***
**The audience's perception of how I present myself—how sure I am of myself and my message.**

Here are some examples of how I exhibit confidence in my verbal and nonverbal behavior:

______________________________________________________________

______________________________________________________________

______________________________________________________________

______________________________________________________________

______________________________________________________________

# PRESENTATION EVALUATION

SPEAKER:

TOPIC:

SPEAKER'S TARGET AUDIENCE:

EVALUATOR:

Directions for the speaker: Evaluate yourself on each point before you present.
Directions for the evaluator: Evaluate the speaker on each point.

| | Good! | Needs work |
|---|---|---|
| **CONTENT** | | |
| Relevant material for audience's knowledge level | | |
| Acknowledgement of audience's wants and concerns | | |
| Sufficient depth in support material | | |
| Interesting examples for audience and situation | | |
| Appropriate visual aids | | |
| **ORGANIZATION** | | |
| Grabs audience's attention | | |
| States clear agenda | | |
| Includes benefit in introduction | | |
| Follows clear organizational plan | | |
| Summarizes essence of main points | | |
| Asks for clear action in conclusion | | |
| Closes with strong final statement | | |
| **DELIVERY** | | |
| Moves comfortably and gestures naturally | | |
| Looks at each member of the audience | | |
| Speaks conversationally and enthusiastically | | |
| Handles visual aids effectively | | |

Overall comments:

Finally, would you hire this person or buy this product or support this proposal?

WORKSHEET

# PRESENTATION EVALUATION TRACKING FORM

**Speaker:**

| | First Speech | Second Speech | Third Speech |
|---|---|---|---|
| | Topic:<br><br>Speaker's Target Audience: | Topic:<br><br>Speaker's Target Audience: | Topic:<br><br>Speaker's Target Audience: |
| CONTENT | • Relevant material for audience?<br>• Acknowledges audience's wants & needs?<br>• Sufficient depth in support material?<br>• Interesting examples?<br>• Appropriate visual aids? | | |
| ORGANIZATION | • Introduction: attention, purpose, benefit, agenda?<br>• Body: limited points, clear plan?<br>• Q&A: controlled & succinct?<br>• Conclusion: summary, action request, final statement? | | |
| DELIVERY | • Moves comfortably, gestures naturally?<br>• Eye contact with entire audience?<br>• Conversational and spontaneous?<br>• Handles visual aids effectively? | | |
| OVERALL | | | |

# Male-Female Communication Issues: Information to Give You an Edge

For the past twelve years, I have focused my professional research on gender differences in workplace communication on the day-to-day, "real world" application of the Strategic Communication Model.

Whether you are a male or female trainer, and whether you are training men or women, knowledge about how men and women communicate can give you an edge. There are two basic premises:

1. Men and women communicate *differently*.
2. Men and women communicate the *same* way but are *perceived differently* by audiences of both genders.[1]

[1]Research on gender differences in workplace communication is predominantly based on American men and women. I exclude three types of studies from my applications:

1) Studies of senior executives—less than 3 percent of whom are women—which conclude that no differences exist
2) Studies of freshman and sophomore college students in controlled environments
3) Studies of intimate relationships

The first is unrealistic for the overwhelming majority of the workplace population; the second and third have little relevance to the corporate environment.)

As your trainees listen, discuss, prepare, present, and evaluate, you will notice some differences in how men and women communicate. The material in this chapter will help you know what to expect from your participants.

- **First important caveat:** These expectations are based on *tendencies* of men and women as cultural groups; individuals may exhibit any combination of "male" or "female" behaviors. Many successful professionals have adopted communication behaviors for specific situations that we normally attribute to the opposite gender.
- **Second important caveat:** The research that supports the information in this chapter is extensive. To explain the "why" of each of these differences would mire you in academic rhetoric that you don't need, but be assured that each and every male and female behavior is documented by credible studies by countless researchers.
- **Third important caveat:** Do not try to digest the many detailed gender differences in this chapter at once. I suggest that you refer to the sections of the Strategic Communication Model that apply to the step of the model that you are preparing. And remember that the information here is designed to guide you in your own preparation and to help you know what to expect from the participants in your workshop—not to suggest definitive solutions. *No man or woman will exhibit every gender-specific trait.*

## GENDER DIFFERENCES IN STEP ONE: ANALYZE THE ENVIRONMENT

Differences between the men and women in your target audience may determine how you analyze your situation and your objectives, so we will begin this application of the Strategic Communication Model with audience analysis.

### Defining Audiences

As you begin learning specific details about your potential audiences, examine potential gender differences to help avoid assumptions and resulting miscommunication. Be very careful to look beyond the obvious as you focus on facts, attitudes, wants, and concerns.

**Facts: the basic differences.** Researchers have identified hundreds of facts about potential differences between male and female individuals who may comprise your multiple audiences. This is a summary of the information that affects workplace communication. Remember that these are *tendencies of groups.* Each characteristic does not apply to every person.

*If your target listener is a man, research indicates:*

- He has been socialized to perform aggressively and to boast of his successes.
- His childhood games taught him that competition is fun and winning is good. He continues to be motivated by competition.

- He views conflict as impersonal and a necessary part of working relationships.
- He has traditionally been afforded attention-getting roles as reflected in his interest in personal benefit and use of the word "I."
- He is impressed by power, ability, and achievement.
- His left-brain orientation produces problem-solving skills that are logical, analytical, factual, and hierarchical.
- He tends to focus on one thing at a time.
- He develops friendships around mutual activities and goals. He builds trust on the basis of actions and accomplishments.
- He is likely to hear only your literal words and miss your underlying emotion. He is not likely to express his feelings through facial expressions.
- His communication style tends to be direct.
- When he succeeds, he attributes it to his ability. When he fails, he attributes the failure to outside circumstances, or he blames someone else.

*If your target audience is a woman, research indicates:*

- She has been socialized to work cooperatively and to be modest about her successes.
- Her childhood games taught her to compromise and collaborate, and she continues to be motivated by affiliation. She competes primarily with herself—that is, with her own expectations of what she should be able to accomplish.
- She takes conflict personally.
- She has traditionally been afforded attention-giving roles as reflected in her interest in the wider needs of the corporate community and use of the word "we."
- She is impressed by personal disclosure and professional courage.
- Her right-brain orientation produces problem-solving skills that are creative, sensitive, and nonhierarchical.
- She has the ability to focus on multiple projects simultaneously. She is probably accustomed to balancing the demands of work, family, home, school, or community issues and thus applies these skills to her job.
- Her friendships are based on personal closeness. She builds trust by sharing both secrets and herself.
- She may be proficient at decoding your nonverbal meanings and is likely to display her feelings through facial expression or body language.
- Her style will tend to be indirect, except with other women of equal rank.
- When she succeeds, she may believe she was lucky. When she fails, she blames herself.

**Differences in male and female attitudes.** The gender of both the speaker and the audience affects your audience's attitudes about you, about your topic, and about being there to receive your information. This affects your relationship with your trainees and their relationships with their audience.

First, consider your audience's attitudes about you. If you are communicating:

- Man to man, you may have instant credibility based on similarity.
- Man to either man or woman, you may start off with a higher perception of credibility than your female counterpart has, especially in terms of expertise, status, and power.
- Man to woman, she may expect that you will not really listen to her. She may also surmise that your idea or plan is based on your independent thinking and that it is an inflexible decision.
- Woman to woman, she may expect you to be friendly, nurturing, and concerned. You may have instant credibility based on similarity.
- Woman to either man or woman, you should expect to have to demonstrate better skills and more experience than a male counterpart does to be perceived as equal in credibility.
- Woman to man, he may expect you to be friendly and nurturing, even passive-dependent. Aggressive behavior and other deviation from his expectations can cause discomfort, confusion, and other negative responses. Or, he may simply disregard you.

Second, consider that men and women may have different attitudes about a particular topic. Your female audience member's greater psychological flexibility makes her more agreeable to change, which is, of course, an element in most persuasive messages. Your male receiver may be more resistant unless he immediately perceives personal benefit.

Third, men and women may respond differently to being your audience; they may have different attitudes about being in your workshop. Your trainees should also expect different attitudes as they present to men and women both in class and at work.

A male listener is more likely to be an autocratic problem-solver. He may resent interrupting his schedule to hear your message unless the other audience members are hierarchically superior, and thus inclusion is a compliment. He will assume that your presentation of a problem (even a hypothetical problem used for illustration in the workshop) is a direct request for a solution.

A female listener is often a team player who is motivated by acceptance and affiliation. She is more likely to appreciate being included in your audience and will respond to your presentation of a problem with support and reassurance. She will offer to share experiences and jointly discuss solutions.

In analyzing attitudes, remember that most people—in your workshop and in the real world—would prefer to be somewhere else, doing something else, with someone else. However, it is likely that the women to whom you speak will be more receptive to you, your topic, and being there than a male counterpart. In other words, men tend to be a "tougher" audience.

**Differences in male and female wants.** The next step in audience analysis involves your determination of what information your audience wants to know. Until you tell the audience what they want to know, they may not be receptive to what they need to know.

A man is likely to want to know the benefit for himself and just what he has to do to win. He will want to know the bottom line—how your plan will help him compete, both as an individual and as an organization.

A woman is likely to want to know the benefit for her workgroup and organization and what she should do to facilitate the process. She may be thinking, "What will be the impact of this plan on the working relationships of the people involved?" She will want to know how your "winning" plan will allow her to provide a win-win situation for everyone rather than a loss for someone else.

**Differences in male and female concerns.** Finally, the consistent concerns of your male and female audience members typify gender differences in your audience. Again, a caveat: *Do not assume* that every man and woman will exhibit each gender-specific trait. In fact, many men and women have adopted situation-specific, successful behaviors of the opposite gender.

You may expect, however, that a careful review of these traits will enhance the depth of your understanding about your audience and therefore increase the probability that you will select the appropriate message content. Remember:

- **Men tend to be most concerned about winning.** They will work as hard as necessary to win over whomever they view as the competition. They fear defeat. They are interested in how the facts affect the bottom line.
- **Women tend to be most concerned with relationships.** They work to do their personal best; their standard of comparison is their own potential. They fear that their successes mean someone else's defeat. They are interested in how the process affects the organization as a whole.

## Defining Situations

As you isolate the situation that now requires you to communicate a message to a particular audience, be aware that both your gender and that of your audience can affect the definition of that problem.

A man may define a situation in terms of outcome. A woman may define the same issue in terms of the people affected. The trick is to define the problem in a manner that will appeal to both the men and the women in your audience. This is no different from appealing to any audience of multiple decision makers: You analyze your audience and select material that addresses their concerns. However, considering the potential of additional issues based on gender is a good "reminder" step in your process.

Then, assess the external climate—what's going on outside of the immediate problem at hand. If your audience is male (or predominantly male), focus more on what is going on in the specific industry (your competition) and in related industries. With predominantly female audiences, focus more on internal issues (like how people can work together to solve a problem).

Finally, evaluate the corporate culture surrounding the problem. A woman may be more sensitive to recognizing if your plan, idea, or a person's behavior is consistent with the corporate culture. Male audience members may not attribute the "fit" of a plan, idea, or person to the effects of culture. Despite their sensitivity to culture, however, women may not be as entrenched in some of the old-line or senior-executive politics, which reduces their comprehensive understanding of the overall culture.

### Defining Objectives

Men and women tend to manage decisions about their message goals differently.

The specific communication purpose should be based specifically on your needs and on your analysis of the target audience. However, men tend to overestimate their likelihood of success, while women tend to underestimate theirs. Your male audiences may allege more knowledge than they actually have, while your female audiences may be modest or even understate their knowledge.

Men and women also tend to have different hidden agendas, and they achieve these objectives differently. Men's goals are likely to be competitive; women's goals may be affiliative. Men may even interrupt when they notice chances to offer information that fulfills their hidden agendas. Women may be more indirect and wait for an opening in which they can offer a conciliatory suggestion.

## GENDER DIFFERENCES IN STEP TWO: CONSIDER YOUR OPTIONS

Even though your training focuses on presentation skills, you should understand the differences in how men and women select and respond to how messages are sent (medium), and when they arrive (timing).

### Media Options: How Messages Are Sent

Here are some expectations about how men and women respond to different verbal media.

*Your male audience member is likely to:*

- Ignore a message circulating on the grapevine, particularly if he receives it from women.
- Expect to discuss important information in a casual conversation, especially when dealing with another man.
- Be defensive about being called to a formal interview, especially if the interviewer is a woman.

- Be annoyed by a phone call that interrupts him, particularly if the caller is a subordinate who does not make the benefit clear.
- Pay little attention in a meeting or formal presentation, unless he understands immediate personal benefit and recognizes that his superiors are included as well.
- Appreciate the technology involved in visual aids, teleconferencing, etc.

*On the other hand, a woman is likely to:*

- Receive a message from the grapevine quickly, particularly if there are other women in the communication network. (Depending on the number of people who repeated the message on its way to her, what she hears may be distorted.)
- Appreciate information received in informal conversation.
- Be intimidated by a formal interview, especially if she is a subordinate who is "summoned" to a man's office. She may expect that the purpose is negative and that she has done something wrong.
- Sound hesitant in response to a phone call that caught her off guard or unprepared.
- Appreciate being included in a problem-solving meeting
- Appear uncomfortable in a teleconference where nonverbal behaviors are altered by technology.
- Offer her attention and positive nonverbal feedback to a formal presentation. This may be an attempt to be supportive and not reflect her true reactions to the speaker and/or message.

### Timing Options: When Messages Arrive

People too often communicate at their own convenience, failing to consider the timing needs of male or female audiences.

A male audience is more likely to be rigid about the deadline he has set for you, even though he is more relaxed about his own deadlines. A female listener is more likely to be considerate of your speaker needs in adjusting a deadline, but she is probably very concerned about keeping hers.

## GENDER DIFFERENCES IN STEP THREE: SELECT AND ORGANIZE INFORMATION

Applying research findings on how men and women listen and process information differently can make you a better trainer and your trainees better speakers. Keep the following gender qualifiers in mind when you are preparing your lectures and when you are discussing general guidelines for selecting and organizing information.

## Planning a Beginning, a Middle, and an End

*When speaking to men:*

- Emphasize personal benefit in the introduction.
- Be succinct with your introduction (but do not delete it!) so that you can quickly get to your major point.
- Reestablish personal benefit in the conclusion.

*When speaking to women:*

- Emphasize the collective benefits for her department or team in the introduction.
- State the organizational plan for your presentation and stick to it.
- Confirm a win-win situation in the conclusion.

## Limiting Your Information

*When speaking to men:*

- Be direct with your main points. Use short, declarative sentences with few qualifiers.
- Include information about the results-oriented impact on the organization's bottom line.

*When speaking to women:*

- Consider an indirect approach to your main points, leading up to your big idea with clear explanations, especially if it is bad news. Don't be too emphatic.
- Include information about the personal impact on individuals and teams. Don't focus entirely on the benefit for the organization.

## Enhancing with Visual Aids, Numbers, and Examples

*When speaking to men:*

- Illustrate your points with clear numbers that will have an impact on the bottom line.
- Avoid personal disclosure to illustrate professional points, especially if you are a female speaker.
- Avoid attempting to impress your male audience with "macho" sports metaphors, especially if you don't fully understand them.

*When speaking to women:*

- Employ personal anecdotes; they will respond to personal disclosure.
- Be careful about using sports or war metaphors, unless you are certain that your audience will appreciate them.

Remember: These are guidelines, not absolutes! You can never assume that an individual is going to think or behave a certain way simply because of gender. However, allow this information to expand your thinking and broaden your considerations as you select the most appropriate and effective material for conveying each message to each audience.

## GENDER DIFFERENCES IN STEP FOUR: DELIVER YOUR MESSAGE

The effects of nonverbal communication are often magnified depending on whether your audience is male or female. Even subtle changes in platform skills can increase effectiveness.

*If you are a man speaking to men:*

- Express your confidence through direct eye contact, but don't worry if the audience does not reciprocate.
- Expect listeners to interrupt, especially if they don't understand something. Appreciate them. Interruptions indicate that your male audience is listening.
- Avoid showing excessive, dramatic enthusiasm for your topic.

*If you are a man speaking to women:*

- Warm up your facial muscles to enhance your ability to express yourself through facial expression.
- Make direct, friendly eye contact with each individual.
- Don't move in too close. Allow enough space for your female receivers to be comfortable. Watch for signs such as stepping away or sitting back in their seats that indicate you are too close.
- Be sensitive to their subtle, nonverbal indications of lack of understanding or need to question, such as a puzzled facial expression. Encourage feedback. They may be hesitant to interrupt you.
- When a female listener offers a comment, communicate a transition from her thought to yours, rather than ignoring her comments or changing the subject.
- Show enthusiasm for your product or idea. Your female audience may interpret a relaxed style as uncaring.

*If you are a woman speaking to men:*

- Warm up your voice to achieve the deepest, most well-projected sound that is possible for you. A lower voice conveys more authority.
- Express your confidence through direct eye contact. Do not look down or at the ceiling.
- Avoid reading or even appearing to read, which reduces the perception of your confidence and therefore your credibility.

- Remove physical barriers, such as lecterns, that diminish your size. Try to stand if your audience is sitting. If you must sit, try to use a seat that puts you at an equal or higher eye level than that of your male audience.
- Employ natural, broad movements to convey confidence. Relax. A perception of nervousness will damage your credibility.
- Avoid tag questions—that is, phrases attached to statements that change the statement to a question ("This is a great idea, don't you think?"). Your male receivers may perceive that you lack confidence about your statement.
- Anticipate interruptions as normal male communication rather than personal attacks or negative feedback.
- Recognize that you may receive little if any active listening, such as smiles or head nodding. This does not mean they are not listening.
- Control your energy and focus your enthusiasm. If you are too dramatic, your male audience may enjoy your performance but miss your message.

*If you are a woman speaking to women:*

- Warm up your facial muscles so that the smile your female audience is expecting will look natural and so that you can freely express the emotional content of your message in your facial expression.
- Reduce space barriers to a minimum by getting as close as you can to your audience. If seated and speaking to an individual or small group, sit on an equal level.
- Take advantage of your female audience's tendency to pick up on the true emotional context of your message. Use your face, hands, and body to express yourself.
- Understand that the nonverbal feedback you are likely to receive may be more polite than expressive of agreement.
- Express your enthusiasm sincerely and personally.

## GENDER DIFFERENCES IN STEP FIVE: EVALUATE FEEDBACK

The differences in the way men and women give and receive feedback may present the most substantial and obvious applications of gender research to the Strategic Communication Model. These differences center on four basic behaviors: the ways in which men and women listen, attribute success and failure, accept responsibility and blame, and filter positive and negative information.

### Behaviors That Affect Feedback

**Listening behavior.** In general, when a woman listens, she offers an active response—that is, she nods her head or says "um-hum" to indicate her attention. A man who is actively listening may simply look directly at the speaker without moving or speaking.

**Attributing success and failure.** When a man succeeds, he believes that it is because of his ability. When he fails, be believes that the situation was simply beyond his control (that is, his assistant didn't prepare the correct report, the client wasn't ready to buy, or the deal wasn't meant to be). When a woman succeeds, she believes that she was lucky, had an excellent support team, or was in the right place at the right time. When she fails, she believes that she simply lacked ability.

Unfortunately, both male and female observers intensify these unbalanced perceptions. Both men and women tend to believe that a man succeeds because of his ability and that a woman succeeds because she has good help or the task is easy.

**Accepting responsibility and blame.** Since a man does not disassociate responsibility and blame, he often refuses to accept them. In addition, he may allow the blame to fall on whoever is willing to accept it.

A woman is quick to say "I'm sorry," meaning that she regrets something happened, not that she regrets she did it. However, she may find herself not only responsible but, by her own admission, at fault.

**Filtering good and bad news.** Male defense mechanisms are better developed than those of women, which means that men tend to be better at shaping reality to their own advantage. As a result, men tend to focus on positive information and filter out the negative, which results in positive self-esteem but little improvement. Women, on the other hand, tend to focus on negative information and filter out the positive, which offers them greater potential for improvement but continues to challenge their self-esteem.

## Gender-Specific Guidelines

These behavioral tendencies generate gender-specific guidelines for soliciting and evaluating feedback from male and female audiences. Use them yourself, and then offer them to your students when the need arises.

*If you are a man receiving feedback:*

- Avoid interrupting; this is your time to listen, not to talk.
- Write down negative comments with the same detail that you note positive comments.
- Ask for examples of negative comments, not just positive ones.
- Look for nonverbal messages that accompany verbal comments.
- Avoid rejecting information with which you do not agree, recognizing that there is some truth in every perception.
- Accept responsibility. You are being held accountable, not being blamed.
- Plan some change in behavior as a result of this feedback.
- Express sincere appreciation for all the feedback, not just the *positive* part.

*If you are a woman receiving feedback:*

- Expect interruptions from the men to whom you are speaking.
- Write down positive comments with the same detail that you note negative comments.
- Ask for positive comments in writing.
- Avoid reading too much into nonverbal information. Pay attention to the actual words, especially if the sender is a man. If the sender is a woman, her nonverbal cues are important, but they should not lead you to exaggerate their meaning.
- Avoid overreacting. Plan to apply some of the feedback, but don't feel obligated to do it all (your minimum response will probably be perceived as a large behavioral change).
- Avoid apologizing, justifying, or giving reasons. Accept the feedback, sort it out, and focus on solutions.
- Express appreciation for all the feedback, not just the *negative* part.

## The Credibility Test

As we discussed throughout this book, the most important element of communication strategy is the perception of credibility by the target audience. Our goal is to achieve credibility, which you will accomplish by applying the Strategic Communication Model. Be aware, however, that men and women who exhibit the same behaviors and who are equal in terms of training, rank, and experience are often not *perceived* as having equal credibility.

Reviewing the Credibility Test in terms of the material in this chapter summarizes the important points about gender differences in workplace communication and will help you select, organize, and present information that will balance the discrepancy in perception.

**Gender differences in the perception of goodwill** (the audiences' perception of the speaker's focus on and concern for them). Women have traditionally been afforded attention-*giving* roles, and men have traditionally been afforded attention-*getting* roles. As a result, both male and female audiences expect that a woman speaker will focus on them more than on herself. The woman who does not meet this expectation loses credibility.

However, if a man offers the same kind of nurturing and attention that is expected of a woman, he receives "extra points." If a female speaker fails to show goodwill through her audience-focus, she will be judged more harshly than would men who behave exactly the same way.

Therefore, a female speaker must meet expectations that she will nurture her audiences. A male speaker, however, has the opportunity to exceed expectations by expressing concern for his audiences.

**Gender differences in the perception of expertise** (the audiences' perception of the speaker's education, knowledge, and experience). Researchers have discovered that even when a man and woman possess equal expertise, both male and female receivers perceive the man as being the more qualified expert.

Therefore, a female speaker must take every opportunity to showcase her knowledge and experience while being very careful not to appear boastful. A male speaker must not exaggerate his knowledge and experience at the risk of seeming unbelievable; audiences will perceive his modesty as charming and persuasive.

**Gender differences in the perception of power** (the receivers' perception of the sender's status, prestige, and success). Researchers have found that when men and women have equal rank, audiences afford higher status to men. Success translates into others' perception of your power as well, but both men and women attribute a man's success to his ability and a woman's success to hard work, good help, and an easy task. In addition, audiences often perceive typically "masculine" behaviors, such as interrupting, controlling conversation, and occupying large amounts of space, as more powerful.

However, women who employ "power behaviors" may confuse or alienate their target audiences. "Feminine" behaviors such as smiling and lingering eye contact often send mixed messages. One audience may perceive a smiling woman as expressing warmth. Another audience may assume that the same woman is being submissive when she smiles, maintains eye contact (perceived as gazing adoringly), and allows her space to be invaded.

Therefore, female speakers must work harder (better data, excellent examples of personal success, more rehearsal, superior visual aids) to be perceived as equal to their male counterparts. Male speakers must perform to the high level of expectation of their audiences.

**Gender differences in the perception of confidence** (the audiences' perception of the speaker's verbal and nonverbal communication skills). Confidence in communication is a *major* expectation in the corporate arena. The confidence with which speakers demonstrate their skills is the most important credibility factor. Both genders have some natural advantages. Men are socialized to lead and thus may be more comfortable in front of groups. On the other hand, women's language skills are often more developed than those of her male counterpart.

Audiences tend to perceive women who do not appear confident in front of people as lacking ability. A less than confident or uncomfortable man, however, may be perceived as endearing, particularly by a female audience.

Therefore, a female speaker must prepare and practice so that both her skills and her confidence are the best that they can be. A male speaker should not allow his natural confidence and extemporaneous abilities to be a rationale for less careful preparation.

## MY STORY

I have personally witnessed examples of every point listed in this chapter. I've been a player in many of the scenes. I expect that you have, too.

So I'd like to share a story about the beginnings of my gender research. (Disclaimer: This story may not be appropriate for all readers. If you are a man with gender-specific distaste for personal disclosure from a woman, you may want to skip to the "Remember" section of the chapter.)

The year was 1984. My daughter was five. She sat with me one night as we watched the Country Music Awards on television. Her father was there; I was at home, ironing his clothes and complaining vehemently with every swipe of the iron. After listening to me complain through a basket of ironing, my daughter finally stated, somewhat perplexed, "But you're the mommy; you're supposed to iron."

Lightning struck. I realized that this child—the most important person in the world to me—believed that her options in life were limited because she was female. And I was her role model—ironing, because I was the mommy. The daddy was working, and it was very exciting work.

A year later I was in my PhD program studying the theories in social psychology about gender differences. My dissertation applied those theories to workplace communication.

My objective as a professor, author, consultant, and trainer has always been to identify the unique strengths of an individual or a company and to capitalize on those strengths to build the perception of credibility. My hidden agenda is to empower women *and men* to expand their communication abilities beyond limiting gender expectations and stereotypes.

Your options may be limited when you communicate—by your audience's needs or by your objectives or by technological logistics—but your options should not be limited because you were born male or female. Masculine communication behaviors need not be competitive, domineering, and insensitive. Feminine communication behaviors need not convey submissiveness, uncertainty, or lack of expertise and power. You can teach your trainees the awareness that will allow them to broaden their skill sets and increase their credibility. And daddies can learn to iron.

## REMEMBER

The problems that arise from differences in the perception of the credibility of men and women in the workplace are complex. So are the solutions. But the first step is to recognize that this is not a woman's issue; it is a corporate issue. Men, women, organizations, and business overall will benefit if men and women of equal rank, training, and expertise are afforded equal credibility.

On an individual level, we must recognize that men and women have been socialized to behave in particular ways and to expect certain behaviors from others. As male and female business communicators, we all have behavioral tendencies. As male and female audiences, we all have biases. Finally, as members of organizations, we have responsibilities. We must recognize both our strengths and weaknesses and those of others to create the greatest possible perception of personal and corporate credibility.

# PART THREE

# EVALUATING THE STRATEGIC PRESENTATIONS COURSE

# Wrapping Up Your Course (So You Get to Do It Again)

Congratulations! You have completed teaching your Strategic Presentations workshop. But you are not quite finished yet. There are two final steps:

1. Solicit and apply feedback from your trainees.
2. Report your results to management and decision makers.

## SOLICITING FEEDBACK FROM YOUR TRAINEES

Build your feedback questionnaire carefully to get good, usable information. I offer these suggestions:

- Request feedback, not evaluation. The distinction may be subtle, but the emphasis should be on insights that can be used to improve future courses. Call your form a "Feedback Form."
- Ask directly for what you want to know. For example, you will probably want a success story to pass on and some specific issues to work on yourself for next time. So ask for this kind of information.

- Ask open-ended questions such as, "What did you like best?" and "What would you change about the course?" Don't use leading, close-ended questions such as, "Most people like this course; was it helpful to you, too?"
- Request specific take-aways such as, "What will you do differently the next time you prepare a presentation?"
- Avoid numerical scales ("On a scale of one to six, how do you rate the content of this course?"). Scaling can be tricky. One person's five is another person's four, and it's difficult to get meaningful insights from such numbers.
- If you want ratings, assign objective descriptions such as, "Exceeded my expectations," "Met my expectations," and "Needed improvement."
- Keep the feedback form simple. If you ask too many questions, you won't get thoughtful answers.

Remember that you have allocated ten minutes on the workshop agenda for this process, so be sure that you stay on schedule. Don't "keep them after school." Their feedback is an important part of the training process, and it could affect your career. Get quality information by making it a meaningful part of the course, not something rushed at the end.

Exhibit 11.1 is an example of one of my favorite feedback forms. It gives me specific answers for comparison, original ideas for improvement, and ammunition for teaching the course again.

WORKSHEET

# COURSE FEEDBACK FORM

**Feedback Form**

As we have discussed in this class, feedback is important for growth and improvement. I value your input and will incorporate your suggestions into my planning for the next workshop.

What did you like best about this workshop?

___

What would you change about this workshop?

___

List three things you will do differently the next time you select information for a presentation:

1. ___
2. ___
3. ___

List three things you will do differently the next time you organize information for a presentation:

1. ___
2. ___
3. ___

List three things you will do differently the next time you deliver a presentation:

1. ___
2. ___
3. ___

Would you recommend this workshop to your colleagues? ___

If yes, what specific elements would be most valuable to your colleagues?

___

If no, please explain why.

___

What is the most important thing you learned in this workshop?

___

Overall, this course (circle one): Exceeded my expectations<br>Met my expectations<br>Needs improvement

Thanks very much!

## REPORTING RESULTS TO MANAGERS AND DECISION MAKERS

Be prepared to share the results of your training with the participants' supervisors and with the decision makers who approved or allocated resources for the training. Remember, your purpose is to present a success story of the course and generate opportunities for repeat sessions. Your report might look something like Exhibit 11.2.

## EXHIBIT 11.2

### SAMPLE MEMO REPORTING ON THE SUCCESS OF A PRESENTATION SKILLS TRAINING COURSE

**Memorandum**

To: John Bigg, Decision Maker
From: Sherron Bienvenu, Training Director
Date: Month xx, xxxx
Re: Results of the Winning Presentations course

Thank you for the opportunity to deliver the Winning Presentations seminar to 24 members of our management group. All of the designated participants attended. I'd like to share some feedback and recommendations.

**Course Feedback**

These are the most frequent answers to each question:

- What did you like best about this workshop?
  1. Relevant information
  2. Practical outlines
  3. Trainer's knowledge
- What would change about this workshop?
  1. Nothing
  2. Allocate more time for individual presentations
  3. Make the group smaller
  4. Add time or take out material
- List three things you will do differently the next time you select information for a presentation:
  1. Benefit for audience
  2. Better audience analysis
  3. Not ask for too much
- List three things you will do differently the next time you organize information for a presentation:
  1. Start with an attention-grabber
  2. Summarize
  3. Reduce my main points

*(continued)*

- List three things you will do differently the next time you deliver a presentation:
  1. Be myself
  2. Not look at the screen so much
  3. Walk around more
- Would you recommend this workshop to your colleagues?
  22 said yes
- If yes, what specific elements would be most valuable to your colleagues?
  1. Focusing on specific audiences
  2. Identifying annoying delivery habits
  3. Improving organization
- If no, please explain why.
  Only one response: They already know this.
- What is the most important thing you learned in this workshop?
  1. I have more to learn
  2. Audiences would rather be somewhere else
  3. Benefit really makes a difference
  4. Always be prepared
- Overall, this course (circle one):
  Exceeded my expectations—18
  Met my expectations—5
  Needs improvement—1

**Recommendations**

Based on this feedback, I suggest that we discuss offering this seminar to other management-level employees. I also recommend that we respond to the request for more time and feedback on individual presentations, either by 1) reducing the group size and extending the workshop to a full day, or 2) offering executive coaching on an as-requested basis. We could pilot an executive coaching program with these 24 participants to measure response and results.

I'll call for an appointment to discuss these issues, and I look forward to our next training programs. Thanks again.

You might also be asked to report on the progress of individual participants. Select appropriate detail from your copy of the Presentation Evaluation Tracking Form (Exhibit 9.3). Remember that your report may have a secondary or hidden audience, so be certain that you are honest but tactful.

Here are some excerpts from a report to a client (Exhibit 11.3). He asked for detail, which I offered. I also reiterated each individual's future goals.

# EXHIBIT 11.3

## EXCERPTS FROM A REPORT ON INDIVIDUAL PRESENTATION SKILLS

Thank you for the opportunity to work with your team in this past week. This is a first-class group of individuals with an extraordinarily high level of knowledge and enthusiasm. I truly enjoyed getting to know them all.

My impressions are summarized for you on the following pages. While perceptions from a three-day relationship in a seminar setting may not be generalized for all workplace behaviors, I'm certain that an individual's styles and tendencies are often consistent in other communication situations. Each participant made significant contributions; almost everyone worked very hard; everyone identified areas that needed attention and work; almost everyone showed measurable improvement. I have encouraged everyone to continue to be aware of potential problem areas and/or continue to work toward established goals. They know what they should do.

### Summary of Individual Evaluations
### Strategic Presentations Seminar

#1: Impressions from their brief persuasive presentation on first day
#2: Impressions from their 10-minute presentation on second day, based on instruction received in first lecture/discussion
#3: Impressions from their 10-minute presentation on third day, based on feedback received from previous presentation

### D.B.

1. Identified some benefits for audience, but appeared somewhat uncomfortable.
2. Obvious preparation. Excellent reasoning and good attempt at organizing difficult material. Nice voice; somewhat stiff style.
3. Worked hard to apply new organization model with a large degree of success. Should try to achieve the comfort level achieved in Q&A throughout presentation. Credible to internal audience.

### B.B.

1. Nice sense of humor and good organization. Needed better benefit and smoother delivery.
2. Obvious preparation. Some excellent material, but struggled with organization. Some creative and effective new visual aids. Lots of vocal variety; very knowledgeable.
3. Obvious preparation. Should continue to work on a clear road map and specific organization. Interesting, comfortable, except with high tech information.

**P.L.**

1. He "won the money" for his opening presentation. Good material; best benefit for audience. Identified some platform skills that needed attention.
2. Obvious preparation. Material well selected for audience. Organization was strong at beginning but didn't hold up. Nice voice; very fluent and confident. Several annoying habits and movements. Good attempt at new slides, but needed edits.
3. Excellent preparation! Material was very focused with wonderful examples. Organization was much improved; he should continue to focus on this. Visual aids were better. He was amazingly more controlled; his energy was focused on his audience. He was knowledgeable, comfortable, confident—very credible and professional. He was very ambitious in his attempts for improvement and met many more goals than I expected in such a short time. I believe he has potential to be one of your best presenters.

**M.N.**

1. Excellent vocal and physical control. Good organization with specific benefits, but long winded.
2. Obvious preparation. Material well selected and organized, with minor suggestions. New visual aids very close to "presentation perfect." Really super to watch and listen to; only small adjustments suggested.
3. I am so impressed with his personal and professional credibility. He is a superior speaker in terms of audience and situation analysis, selection and organization of information and support material, verbal and nonverbal presentation. I also appreciated his contributions to the evaluations and class discussion. Should continue to be a presentation skills role model in your organization.

**P.R.**

1. Kind of quiet. We missed his point.
2. Obvious preparation. Some good material, well focused for audience. Struggled with organization, but pulled it together for a strong close. Sincere style, but quiet; identified several areas for work. Good attempt at visual aids.
3. I couldn't believe this was the same guy. He was really talking to us with lots of enthusiasm, animation, physical and vocal variety, with no loss of sincerity. Very impressive improvement; very professional. Material showed lots of focus on audience, including great examples. Organization and visual aids were much improved; should continue to fine tune. He will have to work to maintain this higher energy style, but I believe that he is both capable and motivated.

**R.S.**

1. Some clever material, but critical of his colleagues in the room, couched in humor.
2. Obvious preparation. Lots of impressive material, but lacked several organizational points. Neat, effective slides, with small suggestions. Articulate, credible, interesting; a couple of habits to break.
3. More impressive material. Much better organization, but still needs some fine tuning. Visual aids were close to perfect. He looks and sounds very professional and knowledgeable. He doesn't need to try as hard as he does to be amusing; he has lots of credibility when he is just being himself.

## MY STORY

I know that feedback helps each of us grow and improve. But I hate it. I get defensive and take it personally. I am definitely not the ideal role model for feedback receptiveness.

Having said that while also recognizing the value of feedback, I had to find a way to get the information I need to improve and try to make it a positive experience. So, I do everything in my power to receive feedback only when I can digest it privately. I only solicit written feedback. I read it, I react (often in all the wrong ways), I get over it, and then I look for the value in it and respond appropriately.

Why, you say, are you telling us this negative story at the very end of this book? Because I want you to know that no one is totally open to all feedback, and that even twenty years of experience won't make it comfortable to have people criticize you. Regardless of how experienced and skillful you become as a presentation skills trainer, you are still going to learn some things each time you do a class. Some of this learning will come the hard way. You'll make mistakes or fail to practice something you've been teaching, and you'll get caught. The whole process of giving and receiving feedback about something as personal as your own communication style will never be painless for you (or your trainees). For some people, this is the hardest part. So work to be open to good feedback and be a role model for your students.

## REMEMBER, ONE LAST TIME

Practice what you teach:

- Learn everything you can about the environment: the current situation, your target audiences, and your objectives with each of those audiences.
- Consider your options: who should send the message, how the message should be sent, and when the message should be sent.
- Use that knowledge to select and organize specific information to meet your objectives with your audiences.
- Deliver your message with a confident, personal style.
- Solicit and evaluate feedback for continued growth and success.

If you follow this powerful model, your messages and your training classes will be focused and delivered with confidence. You will be perceived as credible and therefore persuasive. You will increase your effectiveness as a communicator. You will be a great presentation trainer.

Good job.

# PART FOUR

# STRATEGIC PRESENTATIONS WORKSHOP HANDOUT PACKAGE

- Samples of Title Pages
  —Generic Cover Page #1
  —Generic Cover Page #2
- Course Description
- (Insert your Instructor Bio here)
- My Personal Plan of Action Worksheet
- Copies of Strategic Presentations Workshop Slides (three to a page, with notes lines)
- Audience Analysis Worksheet
- Audience Analysis Worksheet Example (optional)
- Presentation Outline Worksheet
- Presentation Outline Worksheet Example (optional)
- Presenter Credibility Worksheet
- Presentation Evaluation
- Guidelines for Visual Aids
- Guidelines for Inclusive Language

# Strategic Presentations

# Strategic Presentations

# COURSE DESCRIPTION

**Strategic Presentations**

**An In-Depth Workshop for Experienced Professionals**

Strategic Presentations is a workshop designed for business professionals whose speeches are expected to be excellent in terms of focus, organization, support, and delivery.

### Who Should Participate

- Senior executives who represent the company by speaking to clients, shareholders, civic organizations, and employees
- Account executives or marketing managers who make informative and persuasive presentations to other sales representatives, external clients, and end users
- Managers who motivate, inform, or persuade their subordinates, peers, or superiors through demonstrations, speeches, or informal talks

### Workshop Objectives

Through lecture and discussion, oral presentations, professional and self-evaluation (with the help of videotape), and peer feedback, this workshop develops your abilities in the following ways:

- Identify areas of effectiveness and target areas for growth and development in your oral communication skills.
- Increase your listeners' perceptions of your credibility by understanding target audiences and preparing with a focus on the needs and concerns of each audience.
- Design and implement appropriate and powerful visual aids.
- Improve your speaking confidence through objective evaluation and positive reinforcement.
- Enhance your effectiveness in all career responsibilities through relevant application of communication strategies.
- Realistically assess the impact of your communication efforts on other people.

### What Makes Strategic Presentations a Unique Workshop

- Emphasis is based on a Strategic Communication Model:
    1. Learn everything you can about the environment: the current situation, your target audiences, and your objectives with each of those audiences.
    2. Consider your options: Who should send the message, how should the message be sent, and when should the message be sent?
    3. Use that knowledge to select and organize specific information to meet your objectives with your audiences.
    4. Deliver your message with a confident, personal style.
    5. Evaluate feedback for continued growth and success.
- Participants select topics and focus on audiences that accurately reflect real workplace situations. Realistic presentation styles, visual aid options, and audience interaction are encouraged.
- The structure requires only half-day commitments, thus allowing more concentration during the workshop both from and on each participant.
- The workshop leader is an experienced communication specialist with proven success as a corporate trainer.

# MY PERSONAL PLAN OF ACTION

***Research shows that if you use an idea within 24 hours after receiving it, you are more likely to make it a part of your life. So when you hear something you can apply, write it on this sheet immediately. Then hang this sheet where you can't miss it. That way you'll put ideas into action!***

Actions I'll take: When?

## Strategic Presentations



1

## Strategic Communication Model

- Analyze the environment
- Consider your options: media, source, timing
- Select and organize your information
- Deliver your message
- Evaluate feedback for continued growth



2

## Analyze the environment

- Define the situation
- Define your audiences
  - Identify all potential audiences
  - Learn about each audience
- Define your objectives with each audience

3

## Define the situation

- Limit the problem
- Assess the external climate
- Evaluate the corporate culture

 4

## Identify all potential audiences

- Primary--actual
- Hidden--powerful
- Decision maker--relies on second-hand information

 5

## Learn about each audience

- Gather personal and professional facts
- Be aware of attitudes: you, your topic, being there
- Determine their wants over your needs
- Recognize their consistent concerns

 6

## Define your objectives

- Overall goal from mission statement
- Specific purpose of the communication
- Your hidden agenda





## Consider your options

- Media: **how** the message is sent
- Source: **who** delivers the message
- Timing: **when** the message arrives

## Select and organize information

- Review situation, audience, and objectives analysis
- Plan a beginning, middle, end
- Focus on personal benefit
- Limit your information
- Enhance with visual aids, numbers, examples

## Basic outline

- **Introduction**: attention-grabber purpose, agenda, benefit
- **Body**
- **Conclusion**: summary, specific action, final statement



## Decision-making pattern

- Define and limit problem
- Establish checklist of criteria
- Identify possible solutions
- Evaluate solutions, based on criteria
- Select best solution
- Discuss implementation




## Bad news pattern

- Cushion audience
- Bridge with transition
- Deliver bad news
- Explain reasons
- Suggest alternatives
- Rebuild good will

## *STARR pattern*

- Define ***situation***
- Describe your ***task***
- Explain the ***action*** you took
- Show your ***results***
- Offer ***recommendations***

## *Match the visuals to the words*

GOOD VISUAL AIDS

- Appropriate
- Clear
- Consistent
- Dynamic




## *Deliver your message*

- Polish your verbal and nonverbal skills
- Know your material
- Express confidence
- Be yourself

## Polish your verbal skills

- Speak clearly
  - Pronunciation
  - Articulation
  - Volume
  - Pitch
- Speak expressively
  - Emphasis
  - Pace
  - Timing

## Polish your nonverbal skills

- Dress professionally
- Exhibit physical control
  - Your face
  - Your hands
  - Your feet
  - Your space
- Above all else, be enthusiastic

 

## Know your material

- Practice your presentation in sections
- Use notes with discretion
- Manage visual aids smoothly
- Handle questions succinctly
  - Answer the question
  - Offer one piece of support
  - Stop

## *Express confidence*

- In your argument
- In your organization
- In yourself
  - Anti-anxiety techniques
  - Delivery tricks
- In the inevitable disaster



## *Be yourself*

- You are the expert
- You are the one who was asked to speak

## *Evaluate feedback*

- Give feedback
- Solicit feedback
- Receive feedback
- Evaluate yourself: The Credibility Test

## Giving feedback

- Describe something positive
- Express constructive criticism in terms of "I"
- Give a specific example
- Offer an option for a solution
- Close with a positive statement

 

## Soliciting feedback

- Identify people you trust
- Ask them in advance to evaluate you
- Articulate specific issues

## Receiving feedback

- Develop receptive attitudes
- Listen carefully; take notes
- Ask for specifics; paraphrase
- Accept responsibility
- Correct without overreacting
- Find the truth in the perception
- Say "thank you"

 

## *Evaluating yourself: The Credibility Test*

- **Goodwill**: focus and concern
- **Expertise**: knowledge, education, and experience
- **Power**: status, prestige, and success
- **Confidence**: verbal and nonverbal communication





## *You will be successful*

- Analyze the environment
- Consider your options
- Select and organize your information
- Deliver your message
- Solicit and evaluate feedback for continued growth

# AUDIENCE ANALYSIS

Who is my primary audience (actual receiver of my presentation)?

________________________________________

What do I know about him/her/them personally and professionally (age, gender, education, job responsibility and status, civic and religious affiliation, knowledge of subject, cultural background)?

________________________________________

________________________________________

What is his/her/their attitude about me? ____________________

About my subject? ______________________________

About being there to listen to my presentation? ________________

What does my audience *want* to know about my subject?

________________________________________

What do I *need* my audience to know?

________________________________________

What is the *consistent concern* that I always hear from my audience?

________________________________________

What specific information addresses that concern?

________________________________________

Who is my hidden audience? ____________________________

What do I know about him/her/them?

________________________________________

________________________________________

What is the *consistent concern* of my hidden audience?

________________________________________________

What specific information addresses that concern?

________________________________________________

Who is the decision maker? ____________________________

What do I know about him/her?

________________________________________________

What is the *consistent concern* of the decision maker?

________________________________________________

What specific information addresses that concern?

________________________________________________

Other observations: ________________________________

________________________________________________

________________________________________________

# AUDIENCE ANALYSIS EXAMPLE

***(Note and disclaimer: This hypothetical example was based on internet and newspaper articles and developed as a class exercise.)***

Speaker: BigMag Sales Manager

Who is my primary audience (actual receiver of my presentation)?

*Current BigMag sales team*

What do I know about them personally and professionally (age, gender, education, job responsibility and status, civic and religious affiliation, knowledge of subject, cultural background)?

*Diversity in all areas; limited knowledge of the upcoming joint venture with HugeCorp*

What is their attitude about me?

*Open, because they know I have information that they need*

About my subject?

*Skeptical, because they want to know how the joint venture will affect their jobs*

About being there to listen to my presentation?

*Curious, perhaps anxious, because they have been worried and would like to know what the future holds for them and for the company*

What does my audience *want* to know about my subject?

*What's in this joint venture for them. Will jobs be cut, or will employees get more benefits?*

What do I *need* my audience to know?

*I need the sales force to be informed about the change in corporate strategy and about the additional products they will be selling in the future*

What is the *consistent concern* that I always hear from my audience?

*Will this joint venture threaten job security?*

What specific information addresses that concern?

*Employee jobs will remain secure because:*

- *BigMag will remain an equal partner with HugeCorp (each company will maintain separate operations)*
- *Employees may have to sell additional items, which may mean a larger sales force and more job opportunities*
- *The joint venture will likely increase the company profits, which should result in more income and benefits for employees*

Who is my hidden audience?

*Top management of BigMag*

What do I know about them?

*Management is enthusiastic about the joint venture and believes it to be a profitable investment*

What is the *consistent concern* of my hidden audience?

*Management wants to ensure that the sales team is excited and motivated by the joint venture; they know that sales drive profits*

What specific information addresses that concern?

*By addressing the concerns of the sales team, I can get them excited and motivated*

Who is the decision maker?

*Each person in the room; the BigMag Sales team (see info for primary audience)*

# PRESENTATION OUTLINE

## Introduction

- **Attention-grabber.** Based on what I know about my primary audience, what will get his/her/their attention (and also relate to topic and situation)?

______________________________________________

- **Purpose.** As a result of this message, what do I want my audience *to do?*

______________________________________________

- Are there any reasons I should be *indirect* with the purpose of this message (including cultural considerations)? If so, how should I temper my expressed goals?

______________________________________________

- **Agenda.** How am I going to accomplish my objectives; that is, what is my *agenda* for delivering the message?

______________________________________________

- **Benefit for audience.** What's in it for them, *specifically and personally?*

______________________________________________

## Conclusion

- **Summary.** Exactly what do I want my audience *to remember* (the essence of my main points)?

______________________________________________

______________________________________________

- **Specific action.** Exactly what do I want my audience *to do?*

______________________________________________

- **Strong final statement.** What is the last thought I want to leave with them?

______________________________________________

## Body

Choose from these common options:

1. Chronological order for simple, ordered instructions or reports
2. Problem (3 parts) and solution (1 part) for audience with low knowledge
3. Problem (1 part) and solution (3 parts) for audience with high knowledge

   (Note: Your solution should include potential risks.)
4. Current situation and proposed situation (3/1 or 1/3, based on audience knowledge)
5. Inductive format (general to specific) or deductive format (specific to general)
6. Pros and cons (or compare and contrast) for simple analyses or evaluations
7. Decision-making format for complex issues
8. Bad news format for information they do not want to hear
9. STARR format for situation, task, action, result, and recommendations

- Point One: ______________________________

  Support Material (such as statistics or examples):

  ______________________________
- Point Two: ______________________________

  Support Material: ______________________________
- Point Three: ______________________________

  Support Material: ______________________________
- Point Four: ______________________________

  Support Material: ______________________________

# PRESENTATION OUTLINE EXAMPLE

***(Note and disclaimer: This hypothetical example was based on the Audience Analysis Worksheet Example in Chapter Five and developed as a class exercise.)***

Speaker: BigMag Sales Manager

## Introduction

- **Attention-grabber.** Based on what I know about my primary audience, what will get their attention (and also relate to topic and situation)?

  *Here's a look into your future: $$$$$$ (unique opportunity for job advancement and additional income)*

- **Purpose.** As a result of this message, what do I want my audience *to do*?

  *Understand the details of the new partnership between BigMag and HugeCorp*

- Are there any reasons I should be *indirect* with the purpose of this message (including cultural considerations)? If so, how should I temper my expressed goals?

  *no*

- **Agenda.** How am I going to accomplish my objectives; that is, what is my *agenda* for delivering the message?

  *Describe the deal (current situation) and highlight opportunities (proposed situation)*

- **Benefit for audience.** What's in it for them, *specifically and personally?*

  *Increased job satisfaction and financial gain*

## Conclusion

- **Summary.** Exactly what do I want my audience *to remember* (the essence of my main points)?

  *The joint venture will increase both the size of the company and the opportunities for you. As the company profits, so will you.*

- **Specific action.** Exactly what do I want my audience *to do?*
  *Embrace the joint venture as a positive and exciting opportunity.*

- **Strong final statement.** What is the *last thought* I want to leave with them?
  *BigMag + Huge Corp = $$$$$ for YOU!!*

## Body

- **Point One:** *Details of the BigMag/HugeCorp deal (current situation)*

  Support Material (such as statistics or examples):
  *Net worth will be $5 billion*
  *Annual sales will double*
  *Market development opportunities will increase*

- **Point Two:** *Highlight opportunities*

  Support Material:
  *More readers, market appeal (more opportunities for sales)*
  *Higher stock price, profit (more opportunities for income, benefits)*
  *Better image (more opportunities to be proud of your company)*

# PRESENTER CREDIBILITY

*Goodwill:*
**The audience's perception of my focus on them and my concern for them.**

What do I do to show my target audience that I care about them?

________________________________________

________________________________________

What do I do with my friends that illustrates teamwork?

________________________________________

*Expertise:*
**The audience's perception of my knowledge, education, and experience.**

What knowledge, education, and experience do I have that might impress my audience?

________________________________________

________________________________________

This is something that I have accomplished that I am really proud of:

________________________________________

*Power:*
**The audience's perception of my status, prestige, and power.**

What is my rank in the organization, and how might this impress my audience?

________________________________________

________________________________________

What awards or recognitions have I received that might impress my audience?

________________________________________

Here is an example of my personal power (my ability to control my own environment):

___

___

___

Here is an example of my interpersonal power (my ability to influence other people):

___

___

___

Here is an example of my corporate power (my ability to mobilize resources):

___

___

___

Here is an example of relationships that give me "power by association":

___

___

___

***Confidence:***
**The audience's perception of how I present myself—how sure I am of myself and my message.**

Here are some examples of how I exhibit confidence in my verbal and non-verbal behavior:

___

___

___

___

___

# PRESENTATION EVALUATION

SPEAKER:

TOPIC:

SPEAKER'S TARGET AUDIENCE:

EVALUATOR:

Directions for the speaker: Evaluate yourself on each point before you present.
Directions for the evaluator: Evaluate the speaker on each point.

| | Good! | Needs work |
|---|---|---|
| **CONTENT** | | |
| Relevant material for audience's knowledge level | | |
| Acknowledgement of audience's wants and concerns | | |
| Sufficient depth in support material | | |
| Interesting examples for audience and situation | | |
| Appropriate visual aids | | |
| **ORGANIZATION** | | |
| Grabs audience's attention | | |
| States clear agenda | | |
| Includes benefit in introduction | | |
| Follows clear organizational plan | | |
| Summarizes essence of main points | | |
| Asks for clear action in conclusion | | |
| Closes with strong final statement | | |
| **DELIVERY** | | |
| Moves comfortably and gestures naturally | | |
| Looks at each member of the audience | | |
| Speaks conversationally and enthusiastically | | |
| Handles visual aids effectively | | |

Overall comments:

Finally, would you hire this person or buy this product or support this proposal?

# GUIDELINES FOR VISUAL AIDS

Visual aids serve several important purposes. They:

- Provide an outline for your audience so they know where you've been and where you're going.
- Provide an outline for you so you don't have to manage notes.
- Support your oral message with visual images to increase what your audience remembers.
- Support your words with numbers and graphs to increase what your audience comprehends.

Effective visual aids contain four elements: They are appropriate, clear, consistent, and dynamic. They do not have to be complicated or difficult. If you follow these guidelines, preparing visual aids will be enjoyable, and they will serve all their intended purposes.

## Good Visual Aids Are Appropriate

Your visual aids must be appropriate in terms of type and overall design concept.

**Appropriate type.** To select the appropriate type of visual aids, refer again to your Audience Analysis Worksheet. Look for clues that will help you make decisions about colors, illustrations, even choice of words. Pay attention to the expectations about visual aids in your company, based on its corporate culture. Then meet or exceed these expectations. Evaluate the actual venue in which you will be speaking. Check its lighting, room size, and shape. As a basic rule, the bigger the group, the larger and more formal your visual aids. The following chart lists your options with some of the advantages and disadvantages of each.

Remember that *you* are the most important visual element of your presentation, so your audience must be able to see you. Therefore, try to avoid *any option* that requires you to turn off the room lights completely.

**Appropriate design concept.** Always start the preparation of your visual aids by reviewing your analysis of your situation, your audience, and your purpose. Use the details you gathered to make your basic choices of templates, fonts, clip-art styles, colors, and especially words.

If the situation is somber, select serious colors and avoid cartoon clip art. If the audience is multicultural, select easily recognized words and illustrations. If your purpose is motivational, consider themes such as stars, flags, or other icons associated with success. Be creative, but be certain that your overall design is suitable for the occasion, your audience, and your purpose.

**Presentation Visual Aid Options with Advantages and Disadvantages of Each**

| *Option* | *Advantages* | *Disadvantages* |
| --- | --- | --- |
| Models, objects | Offer realism<br>Provide hands-on experience<br>Are appropriate for all cultures | Cannot be seen by large groups<br>Detract from speaker |
| Write-on boards, Flip charts, Write-on transparencies | May be generated by audience<br>Create casual atmosphere<br>Appear spontaneous | Indicate lack of preparation<br>Take time during presentation<br>Require good handwriting<br>Are not appropriate for formal cultures |
| Prepared flipcharts | Transport anywhere | Cannot be seen by large groups<br>Are not appropriate for formal cultures |
| Handouts | Add note-taking capabilities<br>Are appropriate for all cultures | Distract from speaker |
| Computer-generated overhead transparencies | Appear professional<br>Indicate preparation<br>Work in lighted room<br>Require only overhead projector<br>Are appropriate for all cultures | Require back-up bulbs |
| Photographic slides | Show vibrant colors | Require darkened room<br>Preclude returning to an earlier point |
| Video cassettes | Show movement<br>Provide variety | Require video cassette player and monitor large enough for audience to see<br>Are expensive to produce |
| Computer-generated slides presented via computer | Appear professional<br>Indicate technical expertise | May require semi-darkened room<br>Require Liquid Crystal Display (LCD) panel, computer, and overhead projector<br>Technically difficult to trouble-shoot |
| Multimedia productions | Create high-tech atmosphere<br>Appear most impressive of all options | Require complex, advanced computer hardware and software for preparation and presentation<br>Distract from speaker<br>Could overwhelm or intimidate less sophisticated audiences or cultures |

## Good Visual Aids Are Clear

Your visual aids will be clear—that is, they will make sense to your audience—if they follow the outline of your speech and if they succinctly present that outline.

**Follow your outline.** Refer to your Outline Worksheet, and start your preparation by designing one slide for each idea. For example, a basic presentation might have the following slides:

1. Title
2. Attention-grabber
3. Purpose
4. Agenda (road map)
5. Benefit for audience
6. Point #1
7. Support or example for point #1
8. Point #2
9. Support or example for point #2
10. Point #3
11. Support or example for point #3
12. Summary(may be repeat of agenda)
13. Action step
14. Final statement

**Keep it simple.** Limit your slides based on the desired length of your speech. Figure on an average of one slide per minute. (Therefore, the speech for the above example would be approximately 14 minutes.) Then try to limit your material to five lines of copy on each slide. Use no more than seven points for maximum retention. Fewer is better.

## Good Visual Aids Are Consistent

Your slides should be consistent in terms of background, font, structure, capitalization, spacing, and illustrations.

**Background.** Presentation software allows you to select a template for the entire presentation. The more illustrations you plan to use, the simpler your template should be. Choose a style that symbolizes your message or that shows respect for your target audience.

High contrast between background and text provides excellent visibility in a lighted room. Cool, dark colors (blue, purple, black) appear to move away from the audience and warm, light colors (yellow, white) appear to move toward the audience. Therefore, your audience will be more comfortable looking at visual aids with dark backgrounds and light letters. You might try colors that complement your company logo or that reflect the country or culture of your audience.

**Font.** Your fonts should be consistent in terms of size and type.

All titles should be the same size of the same font, and all body copy should be the same size of the same font. For computer-generated transparencies and slides, I suggest a *minimum* size of 28 pt. for body copy and 36 pt. for titles in most standard fonts. Title fonts should be easily recognized as larger.

There are two basic types of fonts: serif (the letters stand on small platforms) and sans serif. Serif is traditional and easier to read. Sans serif looks more contemporary. Titles and body copy may be different from each other, so you might select a sans serif font for your titles (for dramatic effect) and a serif font for your body copy (for easy reading).

Examples of serif:

Bookman Old Style
Garamond
Times New Roman

Examples of sans serif:

Arial
Univers
Comic Sans

**Structure.** When using bullets on slides, the points should be "parallel"—the grammar should be the same. For example: "Analyze the environment, Consider the options, Select information" (each clause begins with a verb). Or: "Media, Source, Timing" (each item is a noun). Or: "Overall goal, Specific purpose, Hidden agenda" (each phrase begins with an adjective).

**Capitalization.** Capitalize sparingly. A mixture of uppercase and lowercase letters creates a more natural and easy-to-read visual. You may print your titles in all capital letters, although you may find that a title in all uppercase takes up too much space. Capitalize only proper nouns and the *first letter* of the first word in each bullet point of body copy. Don't capitalize the first letter of every word; everything will look like a title.

**Spacing.** Decisions about consistency in spacing affect your titles, your body copy, and your bullet points.

Your titles should be in the same spot on each slide (such as centered or flush left or right), although you might need two spacing designs, one for one-line titles and one for two-line titles. (If you are using PowerPoint, start by making a decision on single-line titles in your Slide Master, then adjust for two-line titles. Check for consistency by looking at your work on the Slide Sorter.)

Start your body copy at the same spot on each slide. (Again, in PowerPoint, set this up on the Slide Master, then select View Guides to maintain consistency.) You might have a second starting spot for your slides with two-line titles.

The space between your bullets should be consistent as well. Avoid the urge to spread bullets out if you only have two or three. (Use that extra space for a great illustration.) The space between bullets should be about one-and-a-half times the size of the bullet font. A wrapped bullet point remains single-spaced.

**Illustrations.** Graphs and clip art should be similar in size and type. For example, don't mix cartoon-character clip art with realistic-looking clip art. If you choose photographs, try to use them throughout your presentation. Check your presentation on your Slide Sorter View (in PowerPoint) to be sure your illustrations are about the same size.

You do have several options of where you place your illustrations on your slide. Let the picture and the amount of space you have be your guide. For example, a slide with three long bullets would look good with a wide illustration at the bottom. A vertical illustration that faces right (the picture should always face into the slide to focus your audience's attention on the words) would work on the left side with bullets on the right side.

## Good Visual Aids Are Dynamic

Select powerful words, provocative pictures, impressive charts, and exciting technology.

**Powerful words.** Use action verbs and descriptive adjectives. Don't be shy about using your thesaurus to find exactly the right word, then checking your dictionary to confirm the exact meaning. Be sure your choices are appropriate for your audience's vocabulary.

**Provocative pictures.** The time you invest in finding just the right picture will result in a memorable presentation. Clip-art CDs are inexpensive, scanners are reasonably priced or available at your company, and the Internet is a free treasure chest of incredible pictures, so there is no reason to rely solely on the clip art that comes with your presentation software.

**Impressive graphs.** Illustrations should give your audience the idea, not the detail. Save detailed data for handouts. Select the type of chart based on the relationship you want to show. The following exhibit illustrates examples of charts. But remember: Simplify, simplify, simplify. After you have designed your chart, edit for clarity and succinctness. A common mistake is to put so much information on a chart that the audience doesn't know where to look. The less material on a slide, the better your audience will retain it.

**Exciting technology.** Technology is wonderful—under three conditions:

1. It works.
2. The speaker knows how to work it.
3. It truly enhances the presentation.

## Examples of Charts and the Usage of Each

*Type of chart* | *Example* | *Use*

**Pie**

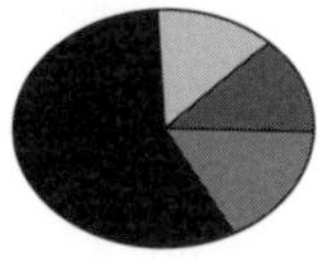

Component comparisons

**Bar**

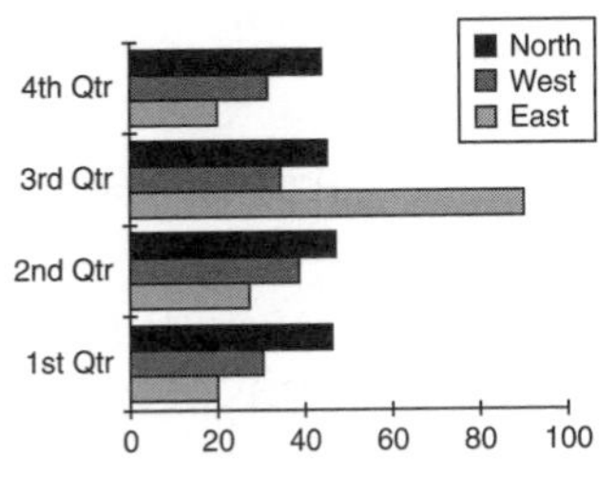


Ranked comparisons

**Column**

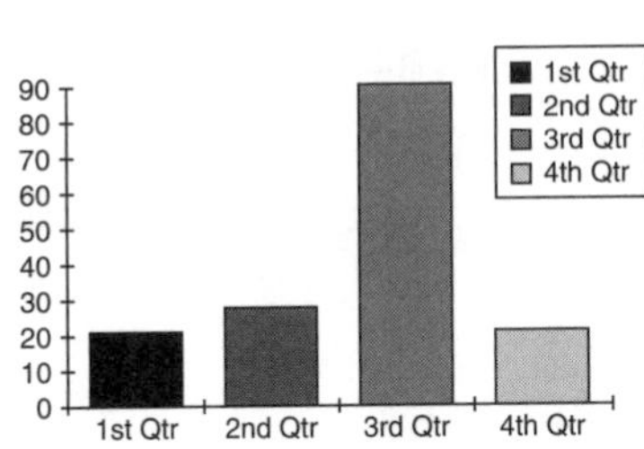


Variation over time

**Line**

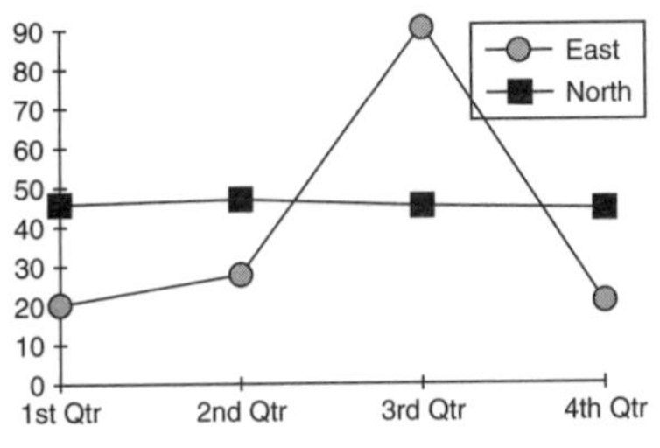


Variation comparison over time

One of the worst things that can happen to a speaker is for the technology to fail. So be sure to test your equipment in advance. Confirm that the computer has enough memory to run your slide show or that the overhead projector bulb is bright enough. Be prepared with whatever extra bulbs, batteries, cords, etc., that you might need.

You will lose credibility even before you start speaking if you don't know how to operate your equipment. If you are using a PowerPoint slide show, rehearse the transitions. Too many speakers are surprised by unexpected sounds or flying bullets. Even something as simple as consistently crooked transparencies can annoy an audience past the point of listening to you. (Hint: Tape a ruler across the top of your projector, then simply slide your transparency frames up against the ruler. You won't even have to look down, and your transparencies will be straight.)

When asked why they added certain "bells and whistles" to their visual aids, too many speakers answer, "Because I could." Not the right answer. Remember that the purpose of visual aids is to support your oral message by helping the audience understand and remember what you say. If they are more impressed by the technology than by your message, you may not accomplish the objectives of your presentation.

---

## REMEMBER

Visual aids provide an outline for both you and your audience, and they enhance the meaning of your presentation so that your audience better understands and remembers what you say. In order to be effective, your visual aids must be appropriate, clear, consistent, and dynamic. But always keep in mind that they are *aids;* they should never distract from you or your message. They should only enhance your presentation.

# GUIDELINES FOR INCLUSIVE LANGUAGE

Inclusive language is that which does not *ex*clude a listener in any way.

The most common business mistakes regarding inclusive language are the use of the word "he" as a generic pronoun and the word "man" as a generic term for human being. These guidelines will help you avoid exclusive and inappropriate word choices.

---

## "HE" AS A GENERIC PRONOUN

In general, avoid *he/she* and *s/he* entirely. Use *he or she* and *her or him* only when absolutely necessary.

Try one of these replacements in a sentence such as *Every worker must wear his or her hard-hat:*

- Convert to plural. *All workers must wear their hard hats.*
- Use second person. *Wear your hard hat.*
- Replace the pronoun (his) with an article (a, an, or the). *Each worker must wear a hard hat.*

---

## "MAN" AS A GENERIC TERM FOR HUMAN BEING

Replacing the generic *man* is not always as easy. For example, referring to a *manhole cover* as *personhole cover* is ridiculous, and *sewer-hole cover* is not much better.

Consider these four categories of language:

- Words that exclude women, such as *chairman and policeman.* (Use words such as *leader* and *police officer.*)
- Words that exclude men, such as *stewardess and actress.* (Use words such as *flight attendant* and *actor.*)
- Words that collectively include men and women but imply only men, such as *manpower and forefathers.* (Use words such as *human resources* and *ancestors.*)
- Words that call inappropriate attention to the person, such as *lady lawyer, female construction supervisor,* or *male nurse.*

Make titles, names of positions or occupations, and common references gender inclusive. Here are some examples, many of which are more specific than the inappropriate version:

| ***Avoid:*** | ***Replace with:*** |
|---|---|
| businessman | worker, manager, executive |
| coed | student |
| congressman | congressional representative |
| delivery man | delivery driver |
| draftsman | drafter |
| firemen | firefighter |
| foreman | supervisor |
| housewife | homemaker |
| husband, wife | spouse |
| mailman | mail carrier, letter carrier |
| man-hours | staff-hours |
| mankind | human beings, humanity, people |
| man-made | manufactured, artificial, synthetic |
| manpower | staff, human resources |
| newsman | reporter |
| repairman | service technician |
| saleslady, salesman | sales associate, clerk, salesperson, sales representative |
| spokesman | representative, advocate, spokesperson |
| waiter, waitress | server |
| watchman | guard, security officer |
| workman | laborer, worker |

# PART FIVE

# COMPLETE SET OF TRANSPARENCY MASTERS FOR STRATEGIC PRESENTATIONS COURSE

# Strategic Presentations

1

# *Strategic Communication Model*

- Analyze the environment
- Consider your options:  media, source, timing
- Select and organize your information
- Deliver your message
- Evaluate feedback for continued growth

# *Analyze the environment*

- Define the situation
- Define your audiences
  - Identify all potential audiences
  - Learn about each audience
- Define your objectives with each audience

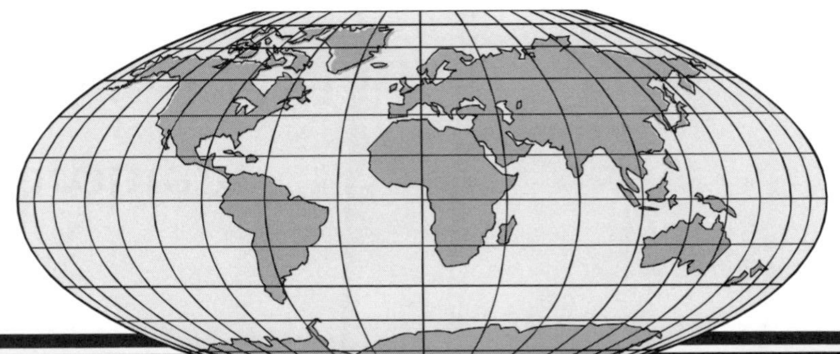

# *Define the situation*

- Limit the problem
- Assess the external climate
- Evaluate the corporate culture

# *Identify all potential audiences*

- Primary--actual
- Hidden--powerful
- Decision maker--relies on second-hand information

# *Learn about each audience*

- Gather personal and professional facts
- Be aware of attitudes: you, your topic, being there
- Determine their wants over your needs
- Recognize their consistent concerns

# *Define your objectives*

- Overall goal from mission statement
- Specific purpose of the communication
- Your hidden agenda

# *Consider your options*

- Media: **how** the message is sent
- Source: **who** delivers the message
- Timing: **when** the message arrives

# *Select and organize information*

- Review situation, audience, and objectives analysis
- Plan a beginning, middle, end
- Focus on personal benefit
- Limit your information
- Enhance with visual aids, numbers, examples

# *Basic outline*

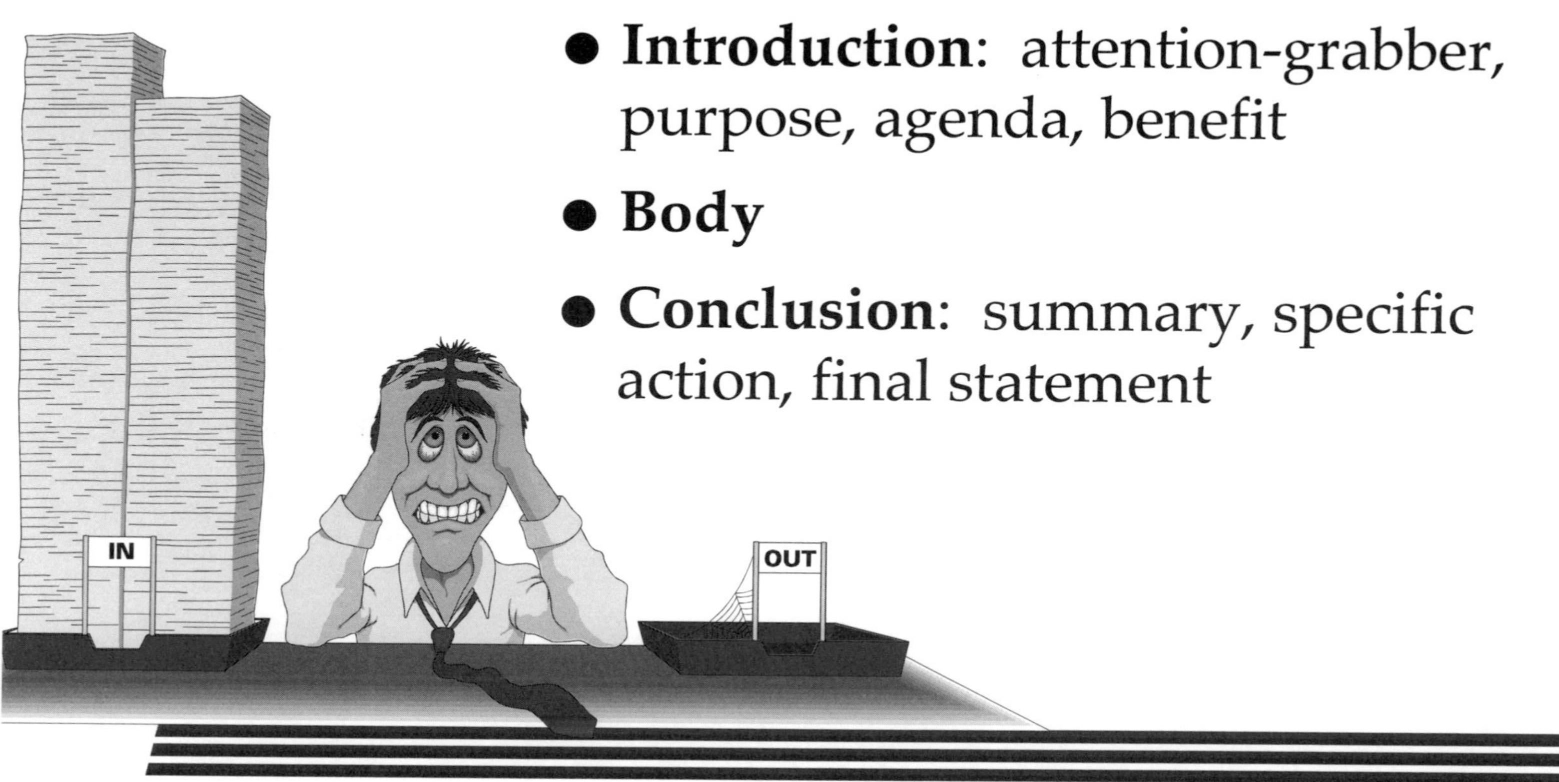


- **Introduction**: attention-grabber, purpose, agenda, benefit
- **Body**
- **Conclusion**: summary, specific action, final statement

# *Decision-making pattern*

- Define and limit problem
- Establish checklist of criteria
- Identify possible solutions
- Evaluate solutions, based on criteria
- Select best solution
- Discuss implementation

# *Bad news pattern*

- Cushion audience
- Bridge with transition
- Deliver bad news
- Explain reasons
- Suggest alternatives
- Rebuild good will

# *STARR pattern*

- Define ***situation***
- Describe your ***task***
- Explain the ***action*** you took
- Show your ***results***
- Offer ***recommendations***

# *Match the visuals to the words*

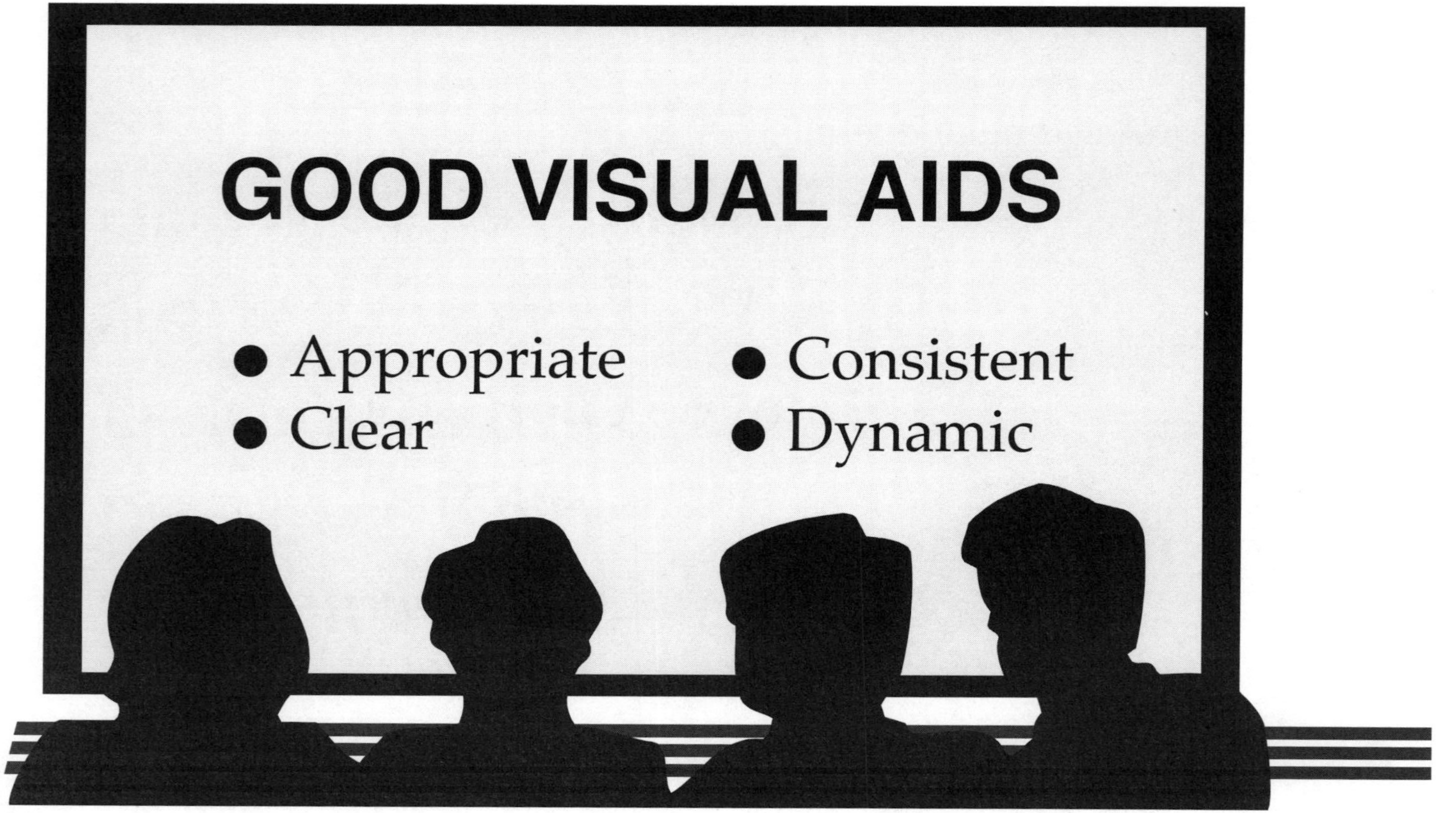

**GOOD VISUAL AIDS**

- Appropriate
- Clear
- Consistent
- Dynamic

# EFFECTIVE PRODUCT ORGANIZATION

- product types are logically arranged
- individual products in the right area
- safe and attractive physical plant

**Example 7.1**

# EFFECTIVE PRODUCT ORGANIZATION

- Logically arranged product types
- Strategically placed individual products
- Safe and attractive physical plant

**Example 7.2**

# Quick Tips for Best Results

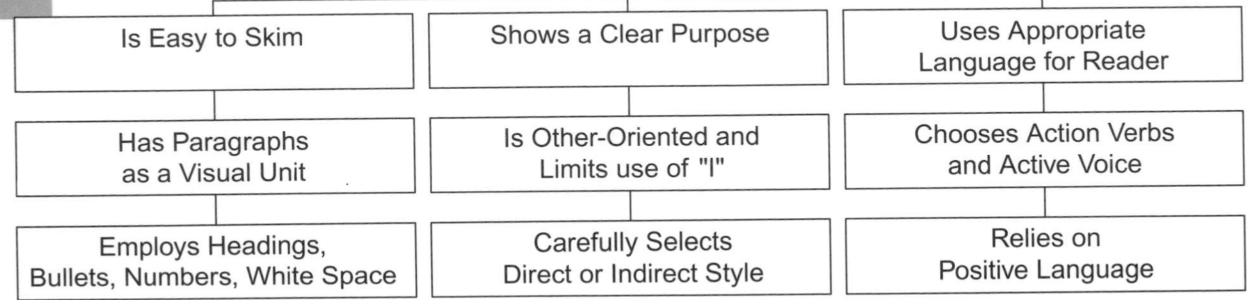


*Business Writing at HugeCorp*

**Example 7.3**

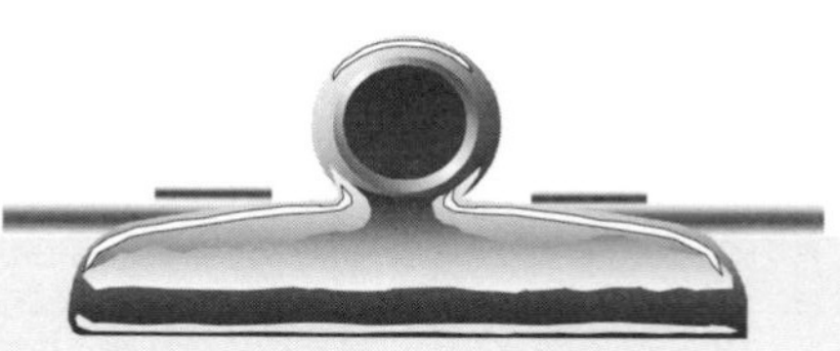

# Write for Results

- ✓ Focus on the reader
- ✓ Write with verbs
- ✓ Choose accurate and appropriate words
- ✓ Be consistent and parallel
- ✓ Check for "skim" factor
- ✓ Proofread out loud

**Example 7.4**

# EXAMPLE: BUYING CALLS, POTENTIAL PROFIT AND LOSS

- Buy a call option for $2, giving you the right to buy a share of stock for $70
- However, your option expires in May
- If the stock price goes above $72 before May, you can exercise your option and make a profit
- The higher the stock price (above $72), the greater your profit
- If the stock price does not go above $72, your loss is limited to $2

**Example 7.5**

# Example: Potential Profit with Call Options

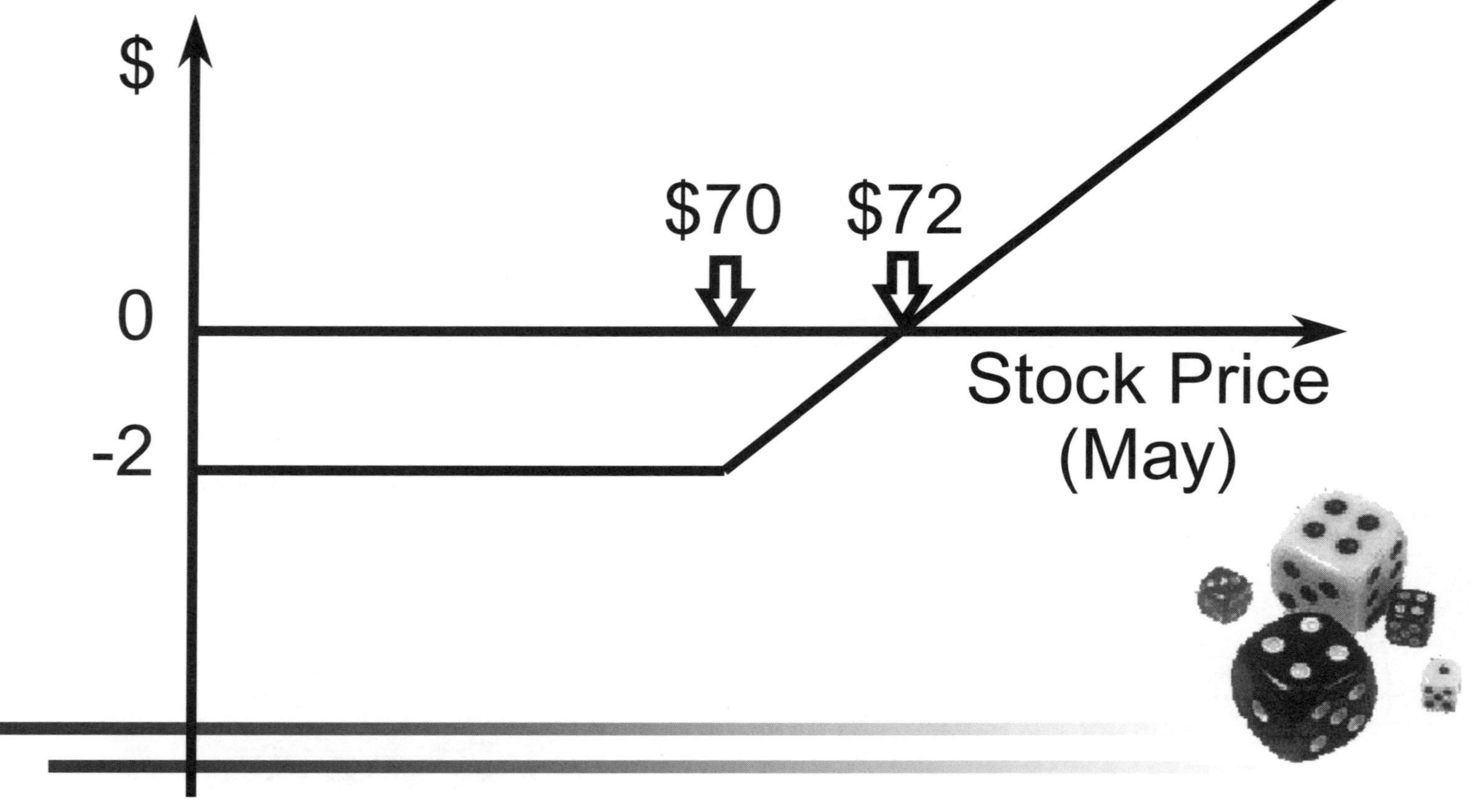


**Example 7.6**

# Summary of C-130J Improvements

- The C-130J Takes Off Faster
- The C-130J Flies Higher and Farther with the Same Load
- The C-130J Cruises at a Higher Speed for a Longer Range with a Heavier Load
- The C-130J is Less Expensive to Maintain Over the Life of the Aircraft

**Example 7.7**

The C-130J
•Faster
•Farther
•Higher
•Smarter
Air Mobility for the 21st Century

**Example 7.8**

# Deliver your message

- Polish your verbal and nonverbal skills
- Know your material
- Express confidence
- Be yourself

# *Polish your verbal skills*

- Speak clearly
  - Pronunciation
  - Articulation
  - Volume
  - Pitch
- Speak expressively
  - Emphasis
  - Pace
  - Timing

# *Polish your nonverbal skills*

- Dress professionally
- Exhibit physical control
  - Your face
  - Your hands
  - Your feet
  - Your space
- Above all else, be enthusiastic

# Know your material

- Practice your presentation in sections
- Use notes with discretion
- Manage visual aids smoothly
- Handle questions succinctly
  - Answer the question
  - Offer one piece of support
  - Stop

# Express confidence

- In your argument
- In your organization
- In yourself
  - Anti-anxiety techniques
  - Delivery tricks
- In the inevitable disaster

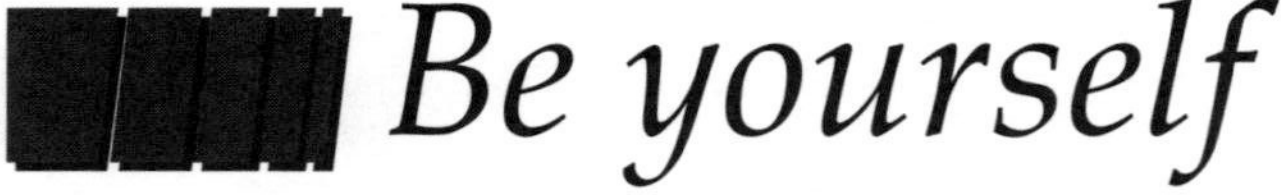

# *Be yourself*

- You are the expert
- You are the one who was asked to speak

# *Evaluate feedback*

- Give feedback
- Solicit feedback
- Receive feedback
- Evaluate yourself: The Credibility Test

# *Giving feedback*

- Describe something positive
- Express constructive criticism in terms of "I"
- Give a specific example
- Offer an option for a solution
- Close with a positive statement

# *Soliciting feedback*

- Identify people you trust
- Ask them in advance to evaluate you
- Articulate specific issues

# *Receiving feedback*

- Develop receptive attitudes
- Listen carefully; take notes
- Ask for specifics; paraphrase
- Accept responsibility
- Correct without overreacting
- Find the truth in the perception
- Say "thank you"

# Evaluating yourself: The Credibility Test

- **Goodwill**: focus and concern
- **Expertise**: knowledge, education, and experience
- **Power**: status, prestige, and success
- **Confidence**: verbal and nonverbal communication

# *You will be successful*

- Analyze the environment
- Consider your options
- Select and organize your information
- Deliver your message
- Solicit and evaluate feedback for continued growth

# APPENDIX A

# The Strategic Communication Model

The Strategic Communication Model provides a foundation for the preparation and delivery of all your oral and written messages. What's attractive about this model is that it is both efficient and thorough—a clean, five-step strategic process for professional, managerial, and corporate communication. An understanding of the model will allow you to be more credible and more persuasive when you present, write, interview, or interact in teams and groups. The model reminds you to:

1. **Learn everything you can about the environment:** the current situation, your target audiences, and your objectives with each of those audiences.
2. **Consider your options:** Who should send the message, how should the message be sent, and when should the message be sent?
3. Use that knowledge to **select and organize specific information** to meet your objectives with your audiences.
4. **Deliver your message** with a confident, personal style.
5. **Evaluate feedback** for continued growth and success.

## STEP 1: ANALYZE THE ENVIRONMENT

The communication environment includes:

- The existing situation
- Your target audiences
- Your desired objectives with those audiences

A thorough understanding of all three of these factors at the beginning of your communication process will provide the foundation for your success. This is a critical step, whether you are planning a sales presentation to an international client, a job interview with a perspective employee, or a written report for your board of directors.

While the communication environment includes situation, audience, and objectives, you must analyze each piece separately. We'll start with the existing situation because the situation often creates the motivation to communicate. Remember, even though you have to look at each piece separately, the situation, audience, and objectives all function in unison.

### Define the Situation

**Limit the problem.** That sounds easy, but isolating the issues at the root of the problem is often difficult. Focus on the distinct cause for the message you must now prepare. Specify the parameters, and simplify the situation to manageable proportions.

**Assess the external climate.** Be aware of what's going on in the specific industry, in related industries, and in the local and global markets that influence the organization and your audiences. Update your research regularly. Things change fast. Our volatile economies create redesigned industries with evolving cultures.

**Evaluate the corporate culture.** The culture of an organization derives from the shared attitudes and beliefs that result in shared behaviors. Tangible indicators of culture found in any company include such things as:

- Formal versus informal communication styles
- Professional versus casual dress codes
- Rigid versus flexible work hours
- Flat versus hierarchical structure
- Entrepreneurial, risk-taking versus conservative, "safe" attitudes

Therefore, a communication strategy that would be appropriate in, say, a highly informal, flexible organization might be completely inappropriate in one that is more formal and structured.

## Define Your Audience

The second part of the Analyze the Environment step includes identifying and learning about the target audiences. Few of us spend enough time on audience analysis, and this step is most likely to contribute details that can make a difference in a highly competitive marketplace. Often, our biggest mistakes are making generalizations and assumptions about our audiences. This model provides questions to ask about your audiences that will take you beyond generalizing and assuming.

**Identify all potential audiences:** primary, hidden, and decision makers. These audience "memberships" can overlap, and there may be no hidden audience at all, but we need to avoid the risk of neglecting the less obvious ones.

The primary audience is the actual individual(s) to whom you speak or write. The hidden audience is an indirect receiver of your message. This audience may not be directly connected with the actual communication purpose or process but may have some power over you. The decision maker is your most important audience, even in situations where this audience gets information second-hand from your primary audience.

**Learn about each audience.** Focus on facts, attitudes, wants, and concerns.

First, gather both professional and personal facts about audience members such as age, gender, cultural background, education, job responsibilities and status, civic and religious affiliations, and knowledge of your topic. Ask yourself a lot of questions. Talk to anyone who may know the people with whom you are about to communicate. Dig for the answers. If your audience comprises individuals inside your organization, you have the advantage of "knowledge by association"—the longer you have worked with people, the more you should know about them.

Second, discover your audience's attitudes about you, your topic, and being there as a receiver of your message. As disillusioning as it may be, the reality is that many people would rather be somewhere else, with someone else, doing something else than sitting there listening to you give a presentation or reading your report.

Third, determine exactly what your audience wants to know. Your job is to give them their "wants" before you ask for your "needs." In fact, one of the biggest communication mistakes is communicating on a "need-to-know" basis. Until you tell them what they *want* to know, they will never hear what you *need* them to know to fulfill the purpose of your message.

Fourth, recognize consistent audience concerns. Most people that you interact with on a regular basis express continuing interest in the same issues. When you have several individuals in your target audience, remember to consider that each might have his or her own consistent concerns.

(Chapter Five includes an Audience Analysis Worksheet with specific questions that will help you get the answers to the kinds of questions addressed above.)

## Define Your Objectives

The third part of the Analyze the Environment step concerns your objectives with each of your audiences. Most messages, no matter how simple, encompass three objectives: an overall goal, a specific communication purpose, and a hidden agenda.

- **Overall goal.** The overall goal should be based on the mission statement of the organization or department. Every message you create should somehow reflect corporate commitments.
- **Specific purpose.** The specific purpose of the communication depends on your needs and on your analysis of the target audiences. Pay particular attention to your audience's level of knowledge about your topic. Remember that your primary audience may know a lot about your subject, but your decision maker may need a review of the background information. Ask yourself, as a result of this communication, exactly what do you want to occur? Here's where people usually make mistakes. They are not *specific* enough.

  The process of persuasion can be visualized as a continuum from zero to ten, where zero represents "I know nothing about this," and ten represents "I'm ready to sign on the dotted line!" Business communicators often assume that their audiences know more than they actually do and ask those audiences to move too quickly up the continuum. Work to accurately assess where your audience is, then set a reasonable objective. You can't get from zero to ten in one speech.
- **Hidden agenda.** Finally, as you complete your decisions about your objectives with the members of your audience, keep in mind that you have a hidden agenda, personal goals to which you are aspiring. *Everybody* has them; it is perfectly normal. Each time you speak or write, you have an opportunity to work toward your goals. Acknowledge that, and factor it into your planning.

## STEP 2: CONSIDER YOUR OPTIONS

Now that you understand your communication environment—the situation, your audience, and your objectives—you can explore the how-who-when options available:

- How the message should be sent (medium)
- Who should deliver the message (source)
- When the message should arrive (timing)

### Media Options: How Should the Message Be Sent?

Technology is providing an almost daily increase in media options. In addition to the traditional presentation, letter, memo, interview, meeting, and telephone call, we also have fax, email, teleconferencing, and the ubiquitous "grapevine" from which to choose when deciding how a message should be sent. An effective communicator evaluates the pros and cons of each option in relation to the situation, the audience, and the resulting goals. Some issues to consider when choosing a medium include:

- Personal or confidential content
- Preparation time
- Convenience of the receiver
- Delivery time required
- Consistency of message for multiple receivers
- Necessity of permanent record
- Appropriateness of nonverbal interaction
- Required response time

Unfortunately, we too often make our choices about how the message is to be sent based on our own communication habits—what's most comfortable for us—rather than on the preferences of our target audiences or the parameters established by the situation.

## Source Options: Who Should Deliver the Message?

When selecting the source—the person to deliver your message—the most important criterion is the perceived credibility of that source by your target audience. In other words, whom will your audience perceive as having the most experience, power, and concern for them?

We often make decisions about the source based on our own needs rather than those of the receiver. We naturally take ownership of a project and then want to personally see it through to completion by delivering the message ourselves to supervisors, clients, and other decisions makers. In truth, however, someone with more perceived credibility with the targeted receiver may be more effective in presenting your message.

## Timing Options: When Should the Message Arrive?

Again, consider the needs of your audience in conjunction with your own communication goals when deciding when to send the message. We too often communicate at our own convenience, which may not be convenient for our audience. Remember that time itself is interpreted differently in other cultures. Time itself conveys meaning.

Additional considerations are sequencing and spacing, particularly with multiple audiences receiving different messages. Complex messages designed for several different audiences require careful scrutiny. Decide which audience is to receive which message in what order. Also consider how much time to allow between messages. The very process of selecting which audience to tell first communicates a strong message in itself.

## STEP 3: SELECT AND ORGANIZE INFORMATION

A common mistake of inexperienced business communicators is to start preparing at this point. We receive an assignment, and we immediately start selecting and organizing information. We try to avoid the requisite first two steps in the model (analyze the environment and consider your options). Since communication is at least 50 percent common sense, you may be able to get by with a lack of analysis some of the time. However, in our current business environment, "getting by" does not provide you with a competitive advantage. And misdirecting information because of poor environment and audience analysis can seriously damage a speaker's credibility.

After you have analyzed environment, considered your options, and are comfortable with your decisions to this point, select an appropriate organizational plan for the information. (Chapter Six includes several basic, flexible organizational plans.) Here are some general guidelines:

- Review your analysis of your situation, audiences, and objectives.
- Plan a beginning, a middle, and an end. An agenda of "tell them what you're going to tell them, then tell them, then tell them what you told them" really works! The purpose is to reinforce, not to be redundant. The consistent message ensures that you will follow through on the purpose of your communication.
- Focus on specific, personal benefit for the individuals receiving the message. Also include benefit for the department or organization.
- Limit your information. Cognitive psychologists tell us that people can remember between three and seven items. Busy business people are more likely to remember only three. If you give too many reasons to buy your product or implement your idea, they may only remember a few of them, and those may not be your most persuasive points.
- Enhance with visual aids, numbers, and examples. No matter how brilliantly you speak or write, your audience will remember your points better if they are supported with pictures and stories that are appropriate for them.

## STEP 4: DELIVER YOUR MESSAGE

For the purposes of our discussion of the Strategic Communication Model, focus on these key issues about your style:

- **Polish your skills.** Develop a style that meets your audience's expectations and is comfortable in its corporate culture. Speak and write clearly and expressively. Display a professional visual image through dress, document layout and design, support materials, and visual aids.
- **Know your information.** Demonstrate that knowledge by thoroughly researching your topics and by rehearsing presentations in advance. Be

prepared to answer questions. Write like you talk—in your own words. Avoid reading; talk to your audience.

- **Express confidence in your material, based on your preparation, and in your company, based on your experience.** Exhibit confidence in yourself, even in the face of adversity.
- **Most of all, be yourself.** Allow your personality to be reflected in all your communication. You are the most important part of your message, and your unique personality is your most valuable platform skill.

## STEP 5: EVALUATE FEEDBACK

Effective communication is an ongoing process of practice and improvement. Yes, you have to get feedback, and no, you won't get any better by presenting over and over in the same way.

Improvement in communication skills is based on realistically evaluating feedback from your target audiences and trusted colleagues. There are four parts to the feedback process:

1. Giving feedback
2. Soliciting feedback
3. Receiving feedback
4. Evaluating yourself with the Credibility Test

Learn to assess accurately when your communication is "working" and when it is not so that you can modify the areas that are less effective. This is particularly tough to do and to teach. Many people consider their communication skills to be a part of their personality, and they take communication skills feedback more personally than feedback on, say, accounting skills. (See the Credibility Test and the Presentation Evaluation form in Chapter Nine.)

### Giving Feedback

If you only offer positive feedback, you are cheating everyone. The speaker or writer will miss the opportunity to learn from matching your perceptions with his/her intentions. Evaluators miss the opportunity to learn from recognizing their own shortcomings through seeing them in someone else's work. The organization will miss the opportunity to improve how ideas are communicated or how products are sold.

Truly useful feedback is that which points out a need for improvement and offers a suggestion for how to make that improvement without demotivating the person who prepared the message. Here is a basic guideline for the organization of this feedback message:

- Describe something positive first.
- Express constructive criticism in terms of "I" (such as "I needed . . ." or "I didn't understand . . .").

- Give a specific example.
- Offer an option for a solution.
- Close with another positive statement.

## Soliciting Feedback

The individual who gives feedback is not the only person responsible for improving communication. To be an effective business communicator, you also need to ask for feedback.

"So, how'd I do?" may not be the best question to ask if you really want thoughtful feedback. You may get "great" and feel better, but you won't get the information you need to learn and grow.

Here are three simple guidelines for soliciting feedback that will help you get better:

- Identify individuals whom you know and trust.
- Ask them *in advance* to evaluate your presentation or report.
- Articulate specific issues that you need them to pay attention to.

## Receiving Feedback

Several extreme behaviors are natural when receiving feedback, such as overreacting, disregarding, or blaming others. None of these reactions will help a speaker improve. Here are some guidelines for developing positive behaviors:

- Develop feedback-receptive attitudes.
- Listen carefully to comments, and take notes in detail.
- Ask for specific information and examples, then paraphrase to confirm meaning.
- Notice nonverbal messages from your audience.
- Correct in the *direction* of the evaluation.
- Accept responsibility.
- Recognize that your audience's perceptions define their reality; show appreciation.

## Evaluating Yourself: The Credibility Test

The most important element of your communication strategy is the perception of credibility. If your audience perceives that you are credible—if it believes you, trusts you, has confidence in you—you will be persuasive. And if you are persuasive, you will get what you want: You will achieve your objectives.

Credibility is the audience's perception of the sender's characteristics. The only reality is the perception of that audience. Your intention doesn't count; how credible you think you are doesn't count. All that matters is what the audience perceives.

Credibility contains four dimensions: goodwill, expertise, power, and confidence. The Credibility Test is your way of double-checking your decisions throughout the Strategic Communication Model.

**Goodwill:** the audience's perception of your focus on and concern for them. Goodwill is your audience's perception of what you think of them. This one is listed first because if you don't pull it off, you won't have a chance with the other three. This dimension is about the audience, not about you. It's the audience's perception of what you think about them—how unique they are, how special they are, how important they are to you.

You will achieve the perception of goodwill from carefully selected information based on your analysis of your audience, situation, and objectives. So obviously, if you haven't thought carefully about the people hearing your presentation, reading your email, or participating in your meeting, you won't be successful on this dimension of credibility. You should consider personal and professional facts, cultural backgrounds, attitudes, and the consistent concerns that they have expressed to you in the past.

**Expertise:** the audience's perception of your education, knowledge, and experience relevant to your topic. Expertise is your audience's perceptions of the facts about you. Of course, this one is a little tricky because you don't want to come off as cocky or conceited.

You will achieve the perception of expertise through illustrative examples that demonstrate your knowledge, education, and experience. It's your chance to share the relevant and impressive facts about yourself.

**Power:** the audience's perception of your status, prestige, and success. Power arises from formal position, association with others who have power, authority you have, and accomplishments. Power is your audience's perception of what other people think about you. Keep in mind that an individual's status, prestige, and success may be perceived differently depending on the specific culture of an organization or industry.

You will achieve the perception of power by selecting material that refers to your rank and illustrates your successes. This is your opportunity to mention any recognition that would illustrate power to this specific audience.

**Confidence:** the audience's perception of how you present yourself—how sure you are of yourself and your message. In addition, people who are perceived as confident are perceived higher on the other three dimensions.

You will achieve the perception of confidence through excellent communication skills, which always include doing your homework and preparing messages tailored to your audiences' needs and concerns. Once the material is right, it's easier to feel confident.

## REMEMBER

So that's it: The Strategic Communication Model, a clean, five-step strategic process for professional, managerial, and corporate communication that will allow you to be more credible and more persuasive when you present, write, interview, or interact in teams and groups. Remember:

- Learn everything you can about the environment: the current situation, your target audiences, and your objectives with each of those audiences.
- Consider your options: Who should send the message, how should the message be sent, and when should the message be sent?
- Use that knowledge to select and organize specific information to meet your objectives with your audiences.
- Deliver your message with a confident, personal style.
- Evaluate feedback for continued growth and success.

Your messages will be focused and confident; you will be perceived as credible and therefore persuasive; and you will increase your effectiveness as a communicator.

# APPENDIX B

# Selling Your Presentation Course

You can practice what you are going to teach by applying the Strategic Communication Model to the issue at hand: Why should anyone invest valuable resources in presentation training? Your goals are to get buy-in from two groups: the managers who are going to support it and the participants who are going to attend it. By going through the model step by step, you will create a successful sales campaign and design a terrific example for your class.

A caveat, however: This is an *example* of how the model can be applied as you sell your course. You would design the actual material for your persuasive messages based on information about the situation, audiences, and objectives in your specific organization.

First, review the steps:

- **Learn everything you can about the environment:** the current situation, your target audiences, and your objectives with each of those audiences.
- **Consider your options:** Who should send the message, how should the message be sent, and when should the message be sent?
- Use that knowledge to **select and organize specific information** to meet your objectives with your audiences.

- **Deliver your message** with a confident, personal style.
- **Evaluate feedback** for continued growth and success.

Now, let's put the model to work.

## STEP 1: ANALYZE THE ENVIRONMENT

The communication environment includes:

- The existing situation (the presenters in your organization are not as good as they need to be)
- Your target audiences (the people who budget for training and those who sign up for classes)
- Your desired objectives with those audiences (get approval, get support, and get a full class)

By carefully thinking about these three elements of the Strategic Communication Model as you begin your communication process, you will provide the foundation for the success of your class.

### Define the Situation

We best define a communication situation by focusing on the specific issue at hand and then looking at the factors in the external climate and internal culture that influence that issue.

**Limit the problem.** The key words here are *isolate, focus, reduce,* and *specify.* You might respond that your "problem" is selling your presentation skills class, arguing that you had narrowed your focus from selling training in general. However, the pivotal issues are likely to be the concerns of the individuals who will approve resources for the training and those who will attend. So let's include the target audiences in the problem statement: "Sell my presentation skills class to management and potential participants at The Company."

**Assess the external climate.** What's going on in the specific industry, in related industries, and in the local and global markets that influence the organization and individuals involved in the message you are preparing? Who else is dealing with the same issues? Who else is doing presentation training? Look for evidence that other organizations, especially those who compete for your clients, are investing in such training. If they are not, what compelling factors in the industry would make such training valuable? How can your organization be the trendsetter? Do your clients expect better presentations?

**Evaluate the corporate culture.** Since the culture of an organization derives from the shared attitudes and philosophies that result in shared behaviors, look for clues that will drive your decisions about what would appeal to your audiences. For example:

- What kinds of presentations are valued by top management?
- Is there client contact that requires organized, focused messages?
- Are company leaders dynamic speakers? If not, do they delegate presentations, perhaps ones they should be making themselves? Are they complacent with their own level of presentation ability? Does this complacency or low skill level pose potential problems or lost opportunities for the company?
- Are company presentations expected to conform to strict time limits and to use a certain type of visual aids?

Whatever you propose should complement and enhance the corporate culture, not clash with it.

## Define Your Audience

The second part of the Analyze the Environment step is to discover details about your audiences that can make your arguments focused and specific. First, we'll decide whom you are targeting and then discuss some questions to ask.

**Identify all potential audiences:** primary, hidden, and decision makers. These audience "memberships" will probably overlap, which makes this exercise a good example for you to use in your class. For example, a manager who participates in allocating training budgets might also be a candidate to sign up for your class.

The primary audience is the actual individual(s) to whom you speak. In this particular situation, you should have two primary groups: managers who approve the training and allocate the resources, and potential participants in the class.

The hidden audience is an indirect receiver of your message. Your actual communication purpose or process may not have an impact on them, but they may have some power over you. Their evaluation of your communication may somehow effect you or your job. Depending on your situation, this hidden audience could be several people, such as your immediate supervisor, someone from another department, or even someone involved in training with another company.

The decision maker is your most important audience. In this situation, in which we are trying to sell the course, your decision makers are probably the same as your primary audience. However, it is possible that someone in the decision-making chain of command will rely on information received secondhand from your primary audience. Be aware that decision makers are likely to have assistants or gate-keepers who may filter your information before it gets to them.

**Learn about each audience.** Focus on facts, attitudes, wants, and concerns of each audience.

First, gather both professional and personal facts about your two groups of primary audiences (managers and participants). Jot down a list of audience members along with as much data as you can think of, including age, gender, cultural background, education, job responsibilities and status, civic and religious affiliations, and knowledge of your topic. The longer you have worked with people, the more you should know about them. If you don't know some key information about an audience member, ask someone who does.

Then, work to discover your audience's attitudes about you, your topic, and being there as a receiver of your message. For example, you may anticipate that managers respect you as a trainer but are uncertain about your ability to teach presentation skills. You may have reason to believe that they may have some understanding about the need for excellent presentation skills, but you're less certain about exactly where they put such training on the priority list. You may expect that they are likely to prioritize you and your proposed presentation training lower than you would like. Be honest in your assessment. Don't paint an unrealistically rosy picture or an unrealistically gloomy one.

Your potential participants may not know you at all. Some of them would rather be thrown into a pit with snakes than to give a speech. And your appeal to them about the class might sound like just another distraction from their "real" work. Your findings might not be encouraging, but identify as many of these important concerns as possible.

Third, determine specifically what your audiences are likely to want to know. Put yourself in their shoes. If you were a manager in The Company, what would you want to know? The managers of my client organizations raise these issues:

- How long are the sessions?
- How many people are in a class?
- How much does it cost?
- Who else is doing this?
- How many people have you trained?

Potential participants want the answers to these questions:

- How long will I be away from my desk?
- How much preparation time is involved?
- Am I being punished or rewarded?
- Do I have to make a speech?

What do you think your audiences will want to know? Remember, until you tell them what they *want* to know, they will never hear what you *need* them to know. Sell your class by meeting their needs for information *they* think is important.

Finally, recognize consistent concerns. Most people that you interact with on a regular basis express continuing interest in the same kinds of issues. You may have generated a long list of concerns as you were thinking about what your audience wants to know. If you work with the same people for an extended period of time, you should know them well enough to identify the issues that always come up about everything. For example, the Chief Financial Officer will always ask about cost, and the Information Systems employee usually requests the option of submitting great slides and not having to stand up and speak. Some people in the organization may view the whole training process as a bunch of touchy-feely nonsense. Again, be realistic in your assessment. Don't be insulted; just factor in these attitudes as you prepare your persuasive effort.

(Chapter Five includes an Audience Analysis Worksheet with questions that will help you get the answers you'll need.)

## Define Your Objectives

The third part of the Analyze the Environment step is to make decisions about your objectives with each of your two primary audiences. Your objectives here, as with most messages, incorporate three factors:

- The degree of congruence between your goal and the mission of the organization
- A specific purpose of this specific message
- Your hidden agenda

**Overall goal.** The overall goal should be based on the mission of the organization or department. Look for written directives such as the mission statement of the organization, the vision statement of the department, or the CEO's yearly goals. Read them carefully for directives that pertain to providing opportunities, striving for excellence, surpassing the competition, or otherwise supporting your argument for training.

**Specific purpose.** Since you have two primary audiences to target with your message, you also have two specific purposes. Determining these two purposes early in your planning process alerts you to the fact that you are going to prepare two distinct messages. Much of the information in both messages will be the same, but you will select some unique material for each audience.

We've determined that your need with both the managers and the participants is basically the same—to sell your course. Inexperienced communicators might stop there. For a truly effective "sell," you must recognize that you are persuading the managers to allocate funds and the participants to sign up.

How much effort you'll need to expend on this phase of planning may depend on how well informed and how well persuaded your audiences are. Let's review the Persuasion Continuum, on which zero represents "I know nothing about this," and ten represents "I'm ready to sign on the dotted line."

At the low end of the scale on the managers' continuum, you may see attitudes like these:

- "I don't think anyone needs presentation training. People either have it or they don't. You can't change human nature."
- "Presentation training may have value for some companies, but not so much for ours."

Toward the middle of the continuum, you might find opinions like these:

- "Presentation skills are useful, but I don't think there's enough money in the budget."
- "Other training is probably more important. We need more computer training, for example."

At the high end of the scale, managers may say things like this:

- "This kind of training can have a dramatic impact on our people's work effectiveness. I see a lot of value here."
- "Sounds perfect! I'll allocate budget and promote your course!"

Your potential students have a similar continuum of attitudes that range from "not interested" to "completely sold":

- "What do you mean, presentation skills training? Who the heck needs that?"
- "I don't really give presentations."
- "I give presentations now and then, but they're not a big deal. I don't think I need to spend time learning any more about this."
- "I give so many presentations, I don't need to be trained in how to do them."
- "I'd love to learn to be less nervous and more effective as a presenter."
- "Sign me up!"

**Hidden agenda.** Finally, as you complete your decisions about your objectives with the managers and participants, keep in mind that you have hidden-agenda, personal goals that you can work toward with this and every message you create. Some hidden-agenda goals my training clients have shared with me include:

- To be perceived by upper management as an innovator
- To be perceived by middle management as a leader
- To be promoted to vice president of human resources
- To be transferred into international sales

Think about your personal goals, then consider information to include in your message that could help you achieve them. For example, information about the positive impact of training on recruiting new employees and motivating existing ones would demonstrate your interest in the entire human resources function.

## STEP 2: CONSIDER YOUR OPTIONS

With a clear picture of the details about your situation (selling your training class), your audiences (managers and potential participants), and your specific objectives with each audience, you can explore the how-who-when options available:

- How the message should be sent (medium)
- Who should deliver the message (source)
- When the message should arrive (timing)

### Media Options: How Should the Message Be Sent?

The culture of a company often dictates the ways that messages are traditionally distributed internally. With the advent of email and the intranet, some organizations' communication methods have become almost paperless. However, I always counsel my clients to choose at least two methods of sending their important messages, based on the habits of the target audiences. For example, even though the majority of employees work almost entirely by computer, key decision makers may pay greater attention to hard copies of some documents—material they can read in the evening at home.

Let's choose several options for selling your course:

- A written proposal for the managers
- A cover memo for the proposal for decision makers
- An email invitation to potential participants
- A memo to participants announcing their selection to participate
- Hard copy and email flyers as reminders

Remember that your most important criterion in choosing how to send your message is what your target audience is most likely to pay attention to, not what is most comfortable for you.

### Source Options: Who Should Deliver the Message?

Your immediate answer is, "This is my course; everything should come from me." In an ideal world, you would be correct with that decision. However, when selecting the source—the person to deliver your message—the most important criterion is the perceived credibility of that source by your target audience. In other words, whom will your audience perceive as having the most experience, power, and concern for them?

Let's look at our four messages again and think about the best person to send them:

- A written proposal (persuasive letter and course description) for the managers. You might be the best person to send this, but also consider that your supervisor might have more clout with the decision maker than you do. That doesn't necessarily mean that the proposal should be signed by your supervisor, but it may be useful if the boss attaches a cover note to grab attention and establish credibility.
- An email invitation to potential participants. Again, this might come from you, but an endorsement from immediate supervisors might help.
- A memo to participants announcing their selection (attach a course description, too). This one definitely would be sent by immediate supervisors. Of course, you would provide it to the supervisors to ensure proper information and tone.
- Hard copy and email flyers as reminders. Okay, this one is all yours. No question.

### Timing Options: When Should the Message Arrive?

Consider the habits of your audience and the culture of your organization as you decide to submit your proposal and advertise your class. For example, what is the budget cycle? Is training for an entire calendar year budgeted the year before, or are these decisions made quarterly or as needed? Do managers hold discretionary funds for training within their departments?

Be careful when you advertise the class to potential participants. If you do it too early, they tend to disregard the message because it lacks urgency. If you wait until the class is almost ready to begin, they may have other obligations. Since this is tricky, I suggest announcing the class two months in advance. If there are major conflicts, someone will alert you. Two months of lead time also allows supervisors to identify candidates for you.

## STEP 3: SELECT AND ORGANIZE INFORMATION

Now it's time to put all your preparation to work. You have gathered a lot of information about your audiences, and you have made several decisions about the types of messages to send.

Let's look at some of the issues that you might have identified and the resulting material to include in your finished messages. The message should include obvious benefit that is both specific and personal.

Managers' issues:

- "Why does the competition have such good speakers?" The competition spends time and money on presentation skills training.

- "The Company is image conscious; everyone wants to look good and sound good." Confident speakers are persuasive and therefore successful. Training teaches you to be confident.
- "Why should I make presentation training a priority?" Knowing everything there is to know only has value if a person can communicate that knowledge to targeted audiences. Presentation training enhances the value of all other training.

Participants' issues:

- "I don't give speeches." Anyone who communicates verbally with clients, supervisors, or employees can benefit from this training. It'll make both your preparation and your presentation easier for you.
- "I don't want to give presentations in front of my colleagues and then be criticized (and possibly humiliated) by a trainer." Everyone has strengths that make them effective. We identify those strengths and encourage you to build on the skills you already have. Criticism can be very helpful since everyone also has things to work on. The training will offer solutions to any communication problems. And, of course, feedback in a well-run course includes both strengths and things to work on. No humiliation. Lots of positive reinforcement.
- "Why me? Am I being punished?" Training is a perk. Being invited means you are valued as an employee. It may even mean you are being groomed for a promotion or additional responsibilities.

Issues from both managers and participants:

- "Training takes time out of the workday and away from clients." Training is a good investment of time and money with a high rate of return. Trained speakers spend less time preparing and meet their objectives more successfully than speakers with little formal training.
- "Who are you?" An experienced trainer with the professional abilities needed to bring participants to new levels of presentations skills. (Always include your bio as part of the proposal, and don't be bashful. If possible, show testimonials from other courses you have run.)

## STEP 4: DELIVER YOUR MESSAGE

Remember these key issues about the actual delivery of your message:

- Polish your verbal and nonverbal skills.
- Know your material.
- Express confidence in your argument.
- Be yourself.

Here are some examples of what your messages might really look like:

# SAMPLE PERSUASIVE MEMO THAT COVERS THE COURSE DESCRIPTION TO DECISION MAKERS

***(Note the application of the basic outline discussed in Chapter Six.)***

**Memorandum**

To: John Bigg, Decision Maker
From: Sherron Bienvenu, Training Director
Date: Month xx, xxxx
Re: Strategic Presentations

Thank you for including me in the New Project off-site meeting yesterday. I appreciated learning more about how all the functional areas are coming together on budget and under deadline. *(Attention-grabber. "Thank you" always works.)*

However, after hearing the various presentations, I recognize that we have an opportunity to enhance the success of the New Project with employees, clients, shareholders, and the media. *(Benefit.)* Everything we are doing is remarkable, but it is not being communicated as effectively as it needs to be. I recommend a series of presentation skills training workshops for everyone who will be talking about the New Project. *(Purpose.)*

I realize that, as a manufacturing firm, we have not made training in "soft" skills a priority, but I can assure you that our competitors are offering presentation skills training to their employees. In the past few months, our sales reps have often commented about the excellent presentations they follow at clients' offices. We can't afford to look or sound anything less than the best. *(Addressing issues of competition and the priority of presentation training.)*

I know you are concerned about time allocation. The training that I am proposing is in three half-day workshops, spaced as much as a week apart. Therefore, employees are not away from their responsibilities for more than four hours in any given day. In addition, participants prepare actual presentations for real audiences, so the time is not invested in hypothetical exercises. *(Addresses issues of time and resource investment.)*

With your approval, I will contact the managers and begin identifying the participants for workshops to begin in about two months. I should be able to train all 100 employees in four to five weeks. The attached course description, which I will circulate to managers and participants, offers more detail. I would be delighted to discuss any additional concerns. *(Addresses concerns about detail and explains attachment.)*

Strategic Presentations is an efficient, effective investment that can only enhance the success of the New Project. *(Summary.)* Please respond at your earliest convenience, and I will immediately begin my preparations. *(Request for action.)* The New Project is just amazing, and after Strategic Presentations training, the message will be as good as the product. *(Strong final statement.)*

# STRATEGIC PRESENTATIONS COURSE DESCRIPTION

## Strategic Presentations

**An In-depth Workshop for Experienced Professionals**
**Designed and Presented by Sherron Bienvenu, PhD**

Strategic Presentations is a workshop designed for business professionals whose speeches are expected to be excellent in terms of focus, organization, support, and delivery.

## Who Should Participate

- Senior executives who represent the company by speaking to clients, shareholders, civic organizations, and employees
- Account executives or marketing managers who make informative and persuasive presentations to other sales representatives, external clients, and end users
- Managers who motivate, inform, or persuade their subordinates, peers, or superiors through demonstrations, speeches, or informal talks

## Workshop Objectives

Through lecture and discussion, oral presentations, professional and self evaluation (with the help of videotape), and peer feedback, this workshop develops your abilities in the following ways:

- Identify areas of effectiveness and target areas for growth and development in your oral communication skills
- Increase your listeners' perceptions of your credibility by understanding target audiences and preparing with a focus on the needs and concerns of each audience
- Design and implement appropriate and powerful visual aids
- Improve your speaking confidence through objective evaluation and positive reinforcement
- Enhance your effectiveness in all career responsibilities through relevant application of communication strategies
- Realistically assess the impact of your communication efforts on other people

## What Makes Strategic Presentations a Unique Workshop

- Emphasis is based on a Strategic Communication Model:
  1. Learn everything you can about the environment: the current situation, your target audiences, and your objectives with each of those audiences.
  2. Consider your options: who should send the message, how should the message be sent, and when should the message be sent?
  3. Use that knowledge to select and organize specific information to meet your objectives with your audiences.
  4. Deliver your message with a confident, personal style.
  5. Evaluate feedback for continued growth and success.
- Participants select topics and focus on audiences that accurately reflect real workplace situations. Realistic presentation styles, visual aid options, and audience interaction are encouraged.
- The structure requires only half-day commitments, thus allowing more concentration during the workshop both from and on each participant.
- The workshop leader is an experienced interpersonal and corporate communication specialist with proven success analyzing, developing, and implementing effective professional, managerial, and organizational communication strategy.

*(Note: Use a summary that best describes your skill set.)*

## About Your Workshop Leader: Sherron Bienvenu, PhD

(*Note:* Use this as a guide to create your own bio. I did this one in sections: academic journals, media coverage, trade publications, consulting and training, and university teaching. Group your accomplishments into appropriate sections as well. You might have company history, education and additional training, company awards, and training or presentation accomplishments.)

Dr. Sherron Bienvenu specializes in application of theories from management communication and social psychology. Her articles have appeared in *The Bulletin of the Association for Business Communication, The Journal of Business Communication, Management Communication Quarterly, The Atlanta Journal and Constitution,* and other publications.

Recognized as a communication expert, Dr. Bienvenu is frequently interviewed by media representatives and has appeared on CNN, CNBC, NPR, and CBS, ABC, and NBC-affiliated television and radio networks.

Most recently, Dr. Bienvenu wrote and appears as on-camera spokesperson in two training videos, "Winning Presentations" and "Winning Credibility," released in early 1998. She also coauthored *CrossTalk: Communicating in a Multicultural Workplace* (Prentice Hall, 1997), a book on communicating in a multicultural environment.

Dr. Bienvenu provides communication counsel for corporations and individuals with expertise ranging from diagnosing organizational communication problems to facilitation of problem-solving and strategic planning. Her corporate clients have included Lockheed Martin Aeronautical Systems, AT&T, Atlanta Gas, MCI, Weeks Corporation, SunTrust Banks, American Cancer Society, Fleet Capital, BellSouth International, and Centers for Disease Control, plus numerous individuals and professional organizations. Her workshops and seminars include a wide range of industries and functional areas: sales, advertising, defense, marketing, healthcare, consulting, broadcasting, real estate, law, education, banking, finance, law enforcement, fundraising, manufacturing, public utilities, and telecommunications.

Dr. Bienvenu began teaching at Goizueta Business School of Emory University in 1982 after a ten-year career in broadcasting and public relations. She manages the communication program and teaches professional and corporate communication strategies to BBA, MBA, and Executive Education students. Her PhD is also from Emory.

## MEMO TO SELECTED PARTICIPANTS FROM THEIR SUPERVISOR

**Memorandum**

To: Selected Participant's Name

From: His or Her Supervisor's Name

Date: Month xx, xxxx

Re: Opportunity to strengthen key communication skills

The rollout of the New Project is going to put all of us in front of customers, shareholders, and key employees in other departments. As a result of this added responsibility, we are planning a series of presentation workshops to enhance both our skills and our confidence.

Your contributions to the New Project are invaluable, and you will certainly be one of the presenters in the months to come. *(Addresses question about being "punished.")* Therefore, you have been selected to participate in this training opportunity.

I am attaching a description of the course and a bio on the trainer. It looks great to me: relevant information, short time commitment, excellent practice with useful feedback, experienced trainer. *(Addresses issues about time, value, and you.)* I know you will benefit.

(Your name) will contact you with scheduling information. Enjoy!

## STEP 5: EVALUATE FEEDBACK

After all your preparation, I'd really like to tell you that your class will now automatically fill to overflowing with enthusiastic participants sent by supportive managers. It might. More likely, however, you will encounter some resistance. Work at understanding this resistance and at listening carefully to feedback you get. Even negative comments—*especially* negative comments—can provide you with insights that build your own communication and training skills. Many of the basic guidelines for receiving feedback apply here, just as they do in a presentation skills class.

### Feedback Guidelines

- Develop feedback-receptive attitudes. Embrace the criticism. Then you know what to fix.
- Listen carefully to comments. Get all of it. Fight the urge to defend your proposal, at least until you have heard everything the person is saying.

- Take notes in detail. Write down both positives and negatives, noting questions and disagreements. This is my personal trick to keep me busy so I won't act defensive.
- Ask for specific information. Ask for examples and try the phrase, "Please tell me more." (This is a tough one—we may not want "more" unless it's positive!) Use the reflective technique to gain more information; for example, "This is what I hear you saying. . . ."
- Paraphrase to confirm meaning. Your perceptions may not be consistent with your evaluator's intentions. For example, "I don't have time for this" could refer to the training classes but may also mean "I have another meeting and can't read this now."
- Notice nonverbal messages. If a person frowns or leans back, stop your pitch and ask about their concerns. It's easier to respond immediately than to let them be distracted by negative thoughts. (And there's always the possibility that that frown is just indigestion.)
- Correct in the direction of the evaluation. Remember, a small correction in the right direction is usually both more appropriate and more feasible. For example, feedback such as "I don't need this" may mean that your reader considers a presentation to be a written document that is read from behind a podium in front of hundreds of people. You can clarify the definition of presentation rather than starting over or quitting altogether.
- Recognize that your audience's perceptions are reality for them. Resist the temptation to reject comments or "correct" perceptions with which you disagree. Respond with appropriate information without discounting their perceptions.
- Say "thank you." It is easier to just leave your proposal in the in-basket than to give you feedback on it. Appreciate the time that your colleagues afford you.

## The Credibility Test

The most important element of your communication strategy is the perception of credibility. If your audience perceives that you are credible—if they believe you, trust you, have confidence in you—you will be persuasive. And if you are persuasive, you will get what you want: You will sell your class to management and fill your class with trainees.

Credibility contains four dimensions of perception: goodwill, expertise, power, and confidence. The Credibility Test provides a systematic way of double-checking your decisions throughout the Strategic Communication Model.

**Goodwill:** the audience's perception of your focus on and concern for them. Goodwill is your audience's perception of what you think of them—how unique they are, how special they are, how important they are to you or your organization.

Achieve the perception of goodwill by carefully selecting information based on your analysis of your audience, situation, and objectives. If your organization is exactly like my example, you've done very well so far. But don't generalize or assume. The messages in the Exhibits are only examples; you should amend them to reflect your specific analysis of your environment.

**Expertise:** the audience's perception of your education, knowledge, and experience relevant to your topic. Expertise is your audience's perceptions of the facts about you.

Achieve the perception of expertise through illustrative examples that demonstrate what you know, where you learned it, and how you have applied your knowledge. It's your chance to share the relevant and impressive facts about yourself. But don't select the same information for everyone; each person will be impressed by different facts.

**Power:** the audience's perception of your status, prestige, and success. Power arises from formal position, association with others who have power, authority you have, and accomplishments. Power is your audience's perception of what other people think about you.

You will achieve the perception of power with material that refers to your rank and illustrates your successes. In the case of selling your class and then teaching it, success is going to be more impressive than status or prestige.

**Confidence:** the audience's perception of how you present yourself—how sure you are of yourself and what you are saying and doing. In addition, people who are perceived as confident are perceived higher on the other three credibility dimensions.

You will achieve the perception of confidence through excellent communication skills, which always includes doing your homework and preparing messages based on your audiences' needs and concerns. Once the material is right, it's easier to feel confident. Since you've done all this, you should feel great.

(Chapter Nine includes credibility worksheets. You might want to fill one out as another exercise in practicing what you are going to teach.)

## MY STORY

The hardest sale I ever had to make was to the business development division of a defense contractor. The decision makers were all former military officers. Both they and the potential participants in my training classes were former pilots of fighter jets, cargo planes, and helicopters. At least 95 percent of the women in the organization were secretaries. As a rule, the women called the men "Mr.," and the men called the women by their first names. The vice president who interviewed me (a career naval officer) was flanked by an entourage. I was outnumbered ten to one.

I had done my homework, but it had only served to prove to me how much I didn't know. I had agonized about a way to make a connection. They had my bio, so they knew about my PhD and my experience (credibility through rank and expertise), and I was doing my best to look confident (sitting up very straight and speaking very calmly). However, I was not in the military, and I had never flown a plane in a war. Even worse, I had visited only one of the sixty-four countries where they marketed their products. So I told a story:

"My father studied aeronautical engineering at LSU. He was drafted into the Army in 1945, sent to Officer Candidate School, and then assigned to an Engineer Construction Battalion. It was, of course, World War II. On D-Day, he landed at Omaha Beach. His mission was to build bridges, but things weren't going as planned, and his company was sent up the beach to clear land mines.

"In spite of how I feel, sitting here this minute, I don't believe that my life is in danger, as my father's was. But I do see a similarity. I have an opportunity here to help you build some bridges. That is my mission. But apparently, you're going to test my ability to clear land mines first."

The silence was deafening. Finally, the vice president leaned forward and said, "Just exactly which companies have you worked for that do exactly what we do?"

I mirrored his nonverbal language, leaned forward to face him, held my breath, crossed my fingers, and said, "None. You are the only company that does exactly what you do." When lightning didn't strike, I added, "But I have trained hundreds of individuals in companies with exactly the same issues and concerns about effective presentations."

My contract with this company ran thirty-seven months. I constantly analyzed my audiences and designed messages to appeal to those audiences, but I won't tell you that it was always easy or that I always got it right. You won't be successful 100 percent of the time either, but applying the Strategic Communication Model gets you where you want to go faster and more often.

## REMEMBER

Review the steps (repetition helps you remember and makes it easier for you to teach):

- Learn everything you can about the environment: the current situation, your target audiences, and your objectives with each of those audiences.
- Consider your options: Who should send the message, how should the message be sent, and when should the message be sent?
- Use that knowledge to select and organize specific information to meet your objectives with your audiences.
- Deliver your message with a confident, personal style.
- Evaluate feedback for continued growth and success.

That's it. You have completed your first application of the Strategic Communication Model. As a trainer, using the Strategic Communication Model will ensure that you appear focused, organized, consistent, and confident. You will indeed be practicing what you are teaching.

# INDEX